Bluetooth Security

For a listing of recent titles in the *Artech House Computer Security Library,*
turn to the back of this book.

Bluetooth Security

Christian Gehrmann
Joakim Persson
Ben Smeets

Artech House
Boston • London
www.artechhouse.com

Library of Congress Cataloging-in-Publication Data
A catalog record for this book is available from the U.S. Library of Congress.

British Library Cataloguing in Publication Data
Gehrmann, Christian
  Bluetooth security.—(Artech House computing library)
  1. Bluetooth technology—Security measures 2. Computer security
I. Title II. Persson, Joakim III. Smeets, Ben
005.8

  ISBN 1-58053-504-6

Cover design by Igor Valdman

© 2004 ARTECH HOUSE, INC.
685 Canton Street
Norwood, MA 02062

International Standard Book Number: 1-58053-504-6

10 9 8 7 6 5 4 3 2 1

Contents

Preface

The simple wireless connectivity Bluetooth technology offers is attractive. Therefore, Bluetooth-equipped devices have found their way into quite different environments and are used for a wide range of applications. However, the security aspects must be carefully analyzed in order to decide whether Bluetooth technology indeed provides the right solution for a particular task.

Several books about Bluetooth wireless technology have been written. While these books are excellent at describing the general functionality of Bluetooth devices, they are not particularly detailed when it comes to the security-related aspects of Bluetooth technology. This book is different in this respect, since it is completely devoted to security matters.

The security features that are defined in the specification are thoroughly discussed and described in the book. Moreover, several interesting facts with respect to this are pinpointed. Specifically, both strong and weak points of Bluetooth security are identified. Additionally, we do not limit ourselves to what directly has been written in the specification. We also want to give some insight into how potential risks and security threats will affect deployment of Bluetooth technology.

This book is divided into two parts. Chapters 1 through 7 (Part I) discuss the security functionality defined on the basis of the Bluetooth version 1.2 specification. However, security is not a feature that comes alone in a system. Security only has a meaning in a certain context. Therefore, the first chapter of this book provides an overview of the Bluetooth system. The communication principles and the security-related functions in the system are covered. For the reader not familiar with security concepts and terminology, the notions and terms used in this book are explained. The security-related functions in the Bluetooth specification are spread over several parts in the system. This explains why it is quite hard to grasp how the different security functions fit together from just reading the specifications. Chapter 2 gives an overview of the whole Bluetooth security architecture. This covers everything from the low-level functions like encryption and authentication to security policies. One core functionality in all security systems is key management. Secure generation, exchange, and distribution of keys is maybe the most challenging task when designing a communication security system. Chapter 3 describes Bluetooth key management. Bluetooth offers link encryption and secure device identification, which is provided by using two different core cryptographic algorithms in various ways. Chapter 4 gives a detailed description of the algorithms and the design principles behind them. Point-to-point encryption is different from sending encryption from one device to several receivers. The Bluetooth standard includes a broadcast encryption function. The broadcast function is described in detail in Chapter 5. Often overlooked by communication system designers are security problems that are not directly related to the communication between devices but are related to the services offered by the devices. Even if strong encryption and identification are provided on a communicating link, the services that utilize the link must use the mechanism in a correct way. This is handled by introducing security policies, which in turn are enforced by access control mechanisms. Chapter 6 describes how this can be dealt with in a Bluetooth system. The last chapter of the first part of this book describes attacks on Bluetooth security. Obviously, it is impossible to correctly judge the appropriate usage of a security technology without a good understanding of the potential weaknesses. We cover all the main reported attacks on the system.

The last three chapters (Part II) of the book focus on possible enhancements to the Bluetooth specification. One of the reported Bluetooth weaknesses is the possibility of tracking the movement of a particular user, so-called location tracking. Chapter 8 describes how location tracking can be avoided by introducing an anonymity mode. Another Bluetooth weakness stems from attacks on the key exchange or pairing. Also, the Bluetooth pairing mechanism can be cumbersome for the user and limit its applicability. In Chapter 9, several key management improvements and extensions are suggested. The final chapter, Chapter 10, deals with a set of Bluetooth applications. We show how security can be provided for these applications using both the standard features and the introduced extensions to these features.

Part I:
Bluetooth Security Basics

1

Introduction

Bluetooth wireless technology is gradually becoming a popular way to replace existing wireline connections with short-range wireless interconnectivity. It is also an enabling technology for new types of applications. In this chapter we give a short background and a condensed description of how the Bluetooth system works. We will focus on details that directly or indirectly relate to security issues and on the functionality that is important in order to understand the concept of the technology. The reference documentation for Bluetooth wireless technology is [1].

1.1 Bluetooth system basics

1.1.1 Background

Bluetooth wireless technology is a short-range radio technology that is designed to fulfill the particular needs of wireless interconnections between different personal devices, which are very popular in today's society. The development of Bluetooth started in the mid-1990s, when a project within Ericsson Mobile Communications required a way to connect a keyboard to a computer device without a cable. The wireless link turned out to be useful for many other things, and it was developed into a more generic tool for connecting devices. A synchronous mode for voice traffic was added and support for up to seven slaves was introduced. In order to gain momentum for the technology and to promote acceptance, the Bluetooth Special Interest Group (SIG) was founded in 1998. The group consists of many companies from various fields. By joining forces, the SIG members have evolved the radio link to what is now known as Bluetooth wireless technology.

3

1.1.2   Trade-offs

Bluetooth wireless technology is targeting devices with particular needs and constraints. The main issues are, as with all battery-powered consumer electronics, cost and power consumption. Consequently, certain design trade-offs have been made between the cost and power consumption on one side and overall performance on the other. For instance, some of the specified requirements for the radio (particularly the sensitivity numbers) are chosen to be so relaxed that it is possible to implement a rather cheap one-chip radio with very few external components (such as filters). The price paid is in a shortening of the range, as it will decrease with decreased sensitivity. On the other hand, some requirements are quite stringent (e.g., adjacent channel rejection) in order to handle interference at frequencies near the intended signal. This helps to keep up the aggregated throughput when many links are running simultaneously. One major design goal is to have the system quite robust in noisy environments. This is because interference rather than range is expected to be the limiting factor of the perceived performance.

In contrast to most other well-known radio standards used for data communication [e.g., Institute of Electrical and Electronics Engineers (IEEE) 802.11b and HIPERLAN], the specification has been written from the beginning with use cases for handheld personal devices in mind. In particular, there is no need to have an infrastructure (i.e., base stations) in place. The flexible Bluetooth master-slave concept was introduced to fit well in a dynamically changing constellation of devices that communicate with each other. Furthermore, due to the wide range of requirements for the traffic types for different applications, Bluetooth can handle various data transport channels: asynchronous, isochronous, and synchronous. It is even possible for a device to mix asynchronous (data) and synchronous (voice) traffic at the same time.

In a radio environment where communication links are set up on request rather than by default (without the need for a centralized infrastructure, as in cellular networks) and where any node is able to communicate with any other node, networking is usually called *ad hoc networking* or *ad hoc connectivity*. As we will discuss later in the book, ad hoc connections impose special requirements for the security functionality for the system. Bluetooth wireless technology is particularly well suited for ad hoc usage scenarios.

1.1.3   Bluetooth protocol stack

The Bluetooth system stack is layered according to Figure 1.1. At the bottom is the *physical layer*, which is basically the modem part. This is where the radio signals are processed. The fundamental limits on sensitivity (range) and interference rejection are set by the radio front end (noise figure) and filters implemented in this layer.

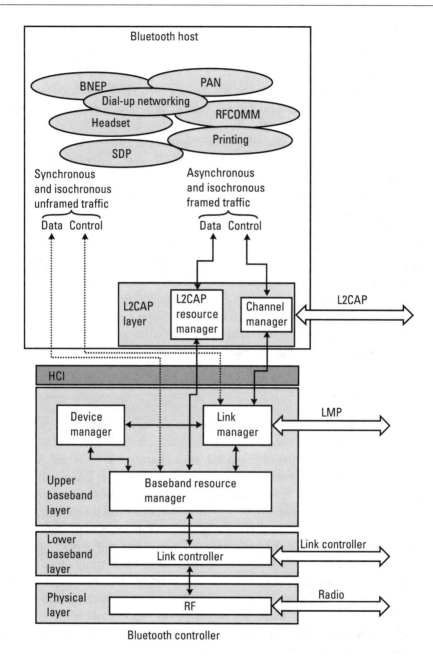

Figure 1.1 A schematic view of the Bluetooth protocol stack architecture. The outermost frame illustrates a possible partition between the host and a module.

Above the physical layer is the *baseband layer*, which is divided into lower and upper parts. In the following, we will not differentiate between these, but simply refer to them as the baseband. It is at this layer that packets are

formatted: creation of headers, checksum calculations, retransmission procedure, and, optionally, encryption and decryption are handled. The *link controller* (LC) is the entity that implements the baseband protocol and procedures.

Bluetooth links are managed by the *link manager* (LM). The devices set up
links, negotiate features, and administer connections that are up and running
using the *link manager protocol* (LMP).

Large chunks of user data need to be reformatted into smaller units before
they can be transmitted over the Bluetooth link. It is the responsibility of the
logical link communication and adaptation protocol (L2CAP) to take care of this.
At this layer it is possible to ask for certain *quality-of-service* (QoS) values one
would like to reserve for the link.

In many cases, the Bluetooth functionality is to be integrated into a host
entity that has computational power but lacks the radio part. For this purpose,
Bluetooth modules handling only the lower layers exist. The entity handling the
functionality of these layers is sometimes referred to as the *Bluetooth controller*.
For instance, a laptop that is perfectly capable of handling higher protocol layers
can embed a module that handles radio, baseband, and L2CAP. In such a setup,
the higher layers that are implemented in the host entity will communicate with
the lower layers of the module through the *host controller interface* (HCI).

1.1.4 Physical layer

Bluetooth radio operates in the license-free and globally available *industrial, scientific, and medical* (ISM) band at 2.4 GHz. Because the ISM band is free, Bluetooth has to share this frequency band with many other systems. Various
wireless communication systems operate in this band (besides Bluetooth, IEEE
802.11b, most notably). Other systems may be defined in the future. One other
common device emitting radio frequency power in this band is found in almost
all homes: the microwave oven. Even though the vast majority of the radiation is
absorbed by the food inside the oven, some of it leaks and will appear outside as
interference. Actually, the leakage may be as much as 1,000 times more powerful than the signal one tries to capture, so this interference cannot be neglected.
Fortunately, the interference is not there all the time (loosely speaking, the
radiation cycle follows the frequency of the power supply) and is not over the
entire frequency spectrum (approximately 15 to 20 MHz of the frequency band
is affected by the microwave oven).

All in all, it is very hard to predict what kind of interference to expect in
the ISM band. To combat this, Bluetooth deploys a *frequency hopping* (FH)
spread spectrum technology. There are 79 channels used, each with a bandwidth
of 1 MHz. During communication, the system makes 1,600 hops per second
evenly spread over these channels according to a pseudorandom pattern. The
idea is that if one transmits on a bad channel, the next hop, which is only 625 μs

later, will hopefully be on a good channel. In general, faster hopping between frequencies gives more spreading, which improves on protection from other interference. However, the improved performance comes at the cost of increased complexity. The hopping rate chosen for Bluetooth is considered to be a good trade-off between performance and complexity.

The signal is transmitted using binary *Gaussian frequency shift keying*. The raw bit rate is 1 Mbps, but due to various kinds of protocol overhead, the user data rate cannot exceed 723 Kbps. Following regulatory bodies in different parts of the world, the maximum transmit power is restricted to 100 mW (or, equivalently, 20 dBm). It is expected that this will give a range of 100m at line of sight. Another power class, where the output power is restricted to 1 mW (0 dBm), is also defined. Radios of this power class are more common in handheld devices, and they will have a range of approximately 10m at line of sight.

One should notice that the specification defines the sensitivity level for the radio such that the raw *bit error rate* (BER) 10^{-3} is met, which translates into the range numbers given above within the specified link budget. It is around this raw BER that a voice link without error-correcting capabilities becomes noticeably distorted. This is a major reason for the choice of the BER 10^{-3} as a benchmark number for the radio specification. However, for data traffic, Bluetooth applies *cyclic redundancy check* (CRC) as well as optional error correction codes. Thus, if the receiver detects a transmission error, it will request a retransmission. The result is that when operating at BER 10^{-3} (and even worse, to some extent), a data link will function quite well anyway. Depending on payload lengths and packet types, the decrease in throughput may even be unnoticed by the user. This is, of course, good for the users, but also for potential eavesdroppers, who may be able to choose a position at a safe distance beyond the specified range for their purposes.

1.1.5 Baseband

Addressing and setting up connections

Each Bluetooth radio comes with a unique, factory preset 48-bit address. This address, known as the *Bluetooth device address* (*BD_ADDR*), constitutes the basis for identification of devices when connections are established. Before any connection can be set up, the *BD_ADDR* of the addressee must be known to the side that initiates a connection. For first-time connections, this is accomplished by having the initiating side collect the device addresses of all nearby units and then individually address the one of interest. This step is known as the *inquiry procedure*. Naturally, once this has been done, the information gathered can be reused without the need for another inquiry at the next connection attempt to one of the known devices.

The first step in finding other devices is to send an inquiry message. This message is repeatedly transmitted following a well-defined, rather short hop sequence of length 32. Any device that wants to be visible to others (also known as being *discoverable*) frequently scans the inquiry hop sequence for inquiry messages. This procedure is referred to as *inquiry scan*. A scanning device will respond to inquiries with its *BD_ADDR* and the current value of its native clock. The inquiry message is anonymous and there is no acknowledgment to the response, so the scanning device has no idea who made the inquiry, nor if the inquirer received the response correctly.

The inquirer gathers responses for a while and can, when so desired, reach a particular device through a *page* message. This message is sent on another length 32 hop sequence determined from the 24 least significant bits of the *BD_ADDR* [these are denoted by *lower address part* (LAP)] of the target device. A device listens for page messages when it is in the *page scan* state. The phase (i.e., the particular position) of the FH sequence is determined from the device's native clock. The paging device has knowledge of this from the inquiry response; thus it is possible for the paging device to hit the correct frequency of the paged device fairly quickly. As already has been stated, the inquiry part can be bypassed when two units have set up a connection before and want to connect again. If a long time has passed since the previous connection, the clocks of the devices may have drifted, causing the estimate of the other unit's native clock to be inaccurate. The only effect of this is that the connection set-up time may increase because of the resulting misalignment of their respective phase in the page hop sequence.

When a page response is received, a rough FH synchronization has been established between the pager and the paged device. By definition, the pager is the *master* and the paged device is the *slave*. The meaning of these terms will be discussed in the next section. Before the channel can be set up, some more information must be exchanged between the devices. The FH sequence, the timing, and the *channel access code* (CAC) are all derived from the master device. In order to fine tune the FH synchronization, the slave needs the *BD_ADDR* and the native clock of the master. This information is conveyed in a special packet sent from the master to the slave. With all information at hand at the slave side, the master and slave can switch from the page hopping sequence (defined by the slave) to the basic channel hopping sequence determined by the master's parameters. Details on this process can be found in [2].

Topology and medium access control

Networks are formed using a star topology in Bluetooth. Not more than eight simultaneous devices can participate in one of these *piconets*. The central node of the piconet is called a *master* and the other nodes are called *slaves*. Thus, a piconet will have exactly one master and at least one but at most seven slaves. The simplest form of piconet is illustrated in Figure 1.2(a). Information exchange within the piconet is done by sending packets back and forth between devices. Full duplex is accomplished using a *time division duplex* mode; that is, the channel access is divided into time slots assigned to the communicating parties. Who gets access to the channel is determined by the piconet master simply by addressing a slave, which will then have the right to send in the next time slot.

Being in connection state, the piconet devices follow a long deterministic FH sequence determined from the master's LAP and native clock. The length of this sequence is 2^{23}, which roughly corresponds to a 23-hour cycle. Following from the fact that a device can only be master of one piconet at a time, every piconet will have different FH sequences. To stay tuned to its piconet, each slave member must continuously adjust for clock drift to the master by monitoring the traffic sent over the channel.

Only master-to-slave and slave-to-master communication is possible. Consequently, slave-to-slave traffic must be relayed via the master. If one particular device is involved in all traffic, there is a risk that it becomes a bottleneck for the data transfer. This property is suboptimal with respect to the aggregated system throughput. However, an important concept in Bluetooth is that all devices have the ability to take the role of either slave or master, so the slaves may choose to create another piconet. Doing so is better for the aggregated throughput, since quite many piconets can actually be operated in parallel before mutual interference cancels the benefits inherent in the parallelism. This principle is shown in Figure 1.2(b).

In principle, a Bluetooth device is allowed to participate in more than one piconet simultaneously, as illustrated in Figure 1.2(c). This is accomplished using time sharing between the different piconets. To accommodate for this, the low-power modes *hold*, *park*, and *sniff* can be used. Without going into detail,

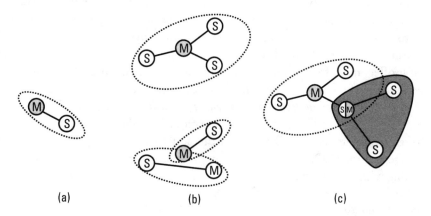

Figure 1.2 Three different piconet constellations: (a) two devices, (b) master relaying versus two separate piconets, and (c) interpiconet scheduling using time sharing.

these modes make it possible for a device to temporarily leave a piconet to do something else (e.g., to sleep to save power or join another piconet). Thus, by having one device be a member of two piconets, it is possible to exchange information between piconets by relaying traffic via the common node. There are, of course, practical problems with this—such as timing issues and fulfilling quality of service when a device is absent from the piconet—but the possibility is given in the specification. One limitation is that a device can only be the master in at most one of the piconets of which it is a member.

Traffic types

Bluetooth wireless technology is designed to handle quite different types of traffic scenarios. Data may be sent without any QoS requirements (referred to as *best effort* traffic); thus, no bandwidth needs to be reserved and there are no requirements for latency or delay. Typically, file transfer and data synchronization fall into this category. Sometimes this traffic is called *asynchronous*. For real-time, two-way communication, the round-trip delay must be kept small, as do variations in the interarrival time of data samples. If not, the quality will be perceived as unacceptable. This type of traffic is referred to as *synchronous*. Typical examples are speech and video conversations. Streaming audio and video falls somewhere in between these categories. Small time variations between data samples is still important, but latency and roundtrip delays are of less interest. Such traffic is called *isochronous*. Bluetooth can handle all these traffic types—it is even possible to mix asynchronous and synchronous traffic between the master and a slave at the same time.

A synchronous link in Bluetooth is referred to as a *synchronous connection-oriented* (SCO) link. It is a point-to-point link between the master and a slave where traffic is sent on slots reserved at regular intervals. Another logical link that carries traffic on reserved slots is called *enhanced synchronous connection-oriented* (eSCO) link. Both these logical links provide constant rate data services by carrying fixed-sized packets on reserved slots over the physical channel. The eSCO link (introduced in Bluetooth version 1.2) is more flexible than the SCO link in that it offers more freedom in choosing bit rates and it is more reliable, as a limited number of retransmissions can take place in between the reserved time slots.

The *asynchronous connection-oriented (logical transport)* (ACL) link is a point-to-multipoint link between the master and all the slaves on the piconet. No reserved slots are used. The master can address an arbitrary slave at any slot not reserved for SCO/eSCO traffic, even one that has a SCO/eSCO logical link running with the master.

Packet structure

A baseband packet consists of an *access code*, a *packet header*, and the *payload*. The access code, which comes first in each packet, is used to trigger and synchronize the receiver. Each piconet uses a unique access code derived from the *BD_ADDR* of the master. Thus, by inspecting the access code, a receiver can determine if a packet is for another piconet. In that case, processing the rest of the packet can be aborted, which will help it save some power. Moreover, as the access code defines where a slot boundary is, it is used to time-synchronize the slave to the master clock. This is necessary, as time drift is inevitable between different devices due to differences in their respective crystal frequencies. Consequently, each slave of a piconet must continuously adjust its clock offset relative to the master clock; otherwise it will eventually lose connection with the master.

The packet header is used to address individual slaves of a piconet. For this purpose, a 3-bit field denoted by *logical transport address* (*LT_ADDR*) is used.[1] The master assigns nonzero addresses to slaves at connection setup, while the all-zero address is reserved for broadcast messages. Apart from this, the packet header conveys information regarding the type of data traffic, flow control, and the retransmission scheme. To increase the robustness of the packet header, it is encoded with a rate $R = 1/3$ repetition code (i.e., each bit is repeated three times).

User data is carried by the payload. The length of this field can vary depending on the type of traffic—from zero bytes (for acknowledgment of received data when nothing needs to be sent in the reverse direction) up to 339 bytes (plus 4 bytes of payload header and CRC). The packet format is depicted in Figure 1.3.

A baseband packet may occupy up to 1, 3, or 5 slots, depending on its type. This allows for having asymmetric data rates in the forward and reverse

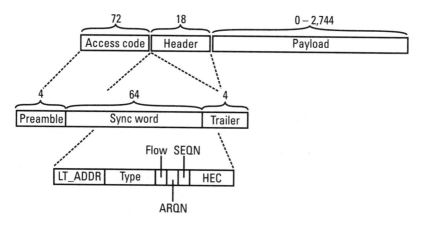

Figure 1.3 Packet format used in Bluetooth. The numbers refer to the number of bits before channel encoding.

---

1. This field was previously denoted by AM_ADDR, but its name was changed in the Bluetooth version 1.2 specification.

directions without the overhead penalty that one-size packets would cause. Error detection may be applied through a 16-bit CRC code. Furthermore, it is possible to apply an error correcting code to the payload—either a rate $R = 1/3$ repetition code, or a (15,10) shortened Hamming code [3] (which has rate $R = 2/3$)—when link conditions are bad. In the Bluetooth specification, one uses the notion *forward error correction* (FEC) for this.

Best effort traffic (i.e., ACL links) without an error correcting code are carried over packets denoted by DH1, DH3, and DH5, where D indicates data, H stands for high rate, and the number is the maximum number of slots occupied by the packet. Similarly, there are DM1, DM3, and DM5 packets (where M stands for medium rate) for packets utilizing the shortened Hamming code. Using these packet types, it is possible to have user data rates ranging from 108.8 Kbps (symmetric, DM1) to 723.2 Kbps (forward) and 57.6 Kbps (reverse) for DH5 packets. The achievable data rates using ACL packets are summarized in Table 1.1.

For synchronous traffic, there are the HV1, HV2, and HV3 [where H stands for high-quality (referring to the relatively high bit rate available for speech coding) and V stands for voice] packets of 10, 20, and 30 information bytes, respectively. These one-slot packets have no CRC applied to the payload and are typically used to carry voice traffic. The achievable rate for all HV packets is 64 Kbps. The HV1 packet is protected by the rate $R = 1/3$ repetition code, the HV2 packet is protected by the rate $R = 2/3$ Hamming code, and the HV3 packet has no error correcting code applied. There is also a DV packet which consists of two parts—one carrying 10 bytes of voice data (no CRC) and one

Table 1.1
Summary of ACL Packets and Their Achievable Data Rates (in Kbps)

Type	Payload (Information Bytes)	FEC	CRC	Symmetric Max. Rate	Asymmetric Max. Rate Forward	Reverse
DM1	0–17	2/3	Yes	108.8	108.8	108.8
DH1	0–27	No	Yes	172.8	172.8	172.8
DM3	0–121	2/3	Yes	258.1	387.2	54.4
DH3	0–183	No	Yes	390.4	585.6	86.4
DM5	0–224	2/3	Yes	286.7	477.8	36.3
DH5	0–339	No	Yes	433.9	723.2	57.6
AUX1	0–29	No	No	185.6	185.6	185.6

carrying asynchronous user data (0 to 9 bytes) for which CRC is applied. The voice part also offers 64 Kbps. In addition to these, the eSCO logical transport is mapped on EV3, EV4, and EV5 packets. All these have a CRC, which implies that retransmission is possible if no acknowledgment has been received within the retransmission window. The EV4 also applies the error correcting code to the payload. For these packets, the achievable rates are 96, 192, and 288 Kbps, respectively. The rates that are supported for synchronous traffic are summarized in Table 1.2.

1.1.6 Link manager protocol

It is the link manager that is responsible for the control of the Bluetooth link. That includes all tasks related to the setup, detachment, or configuration of a link. The LM is also responsible for exchanging security-related messages. The LMs in different units exchange control messages using the LMP. A large set of control messages or LMP *protocol data units* (PDU) have been defined. Many of these are security related and some PDUs are used to carry the information needed at pairing and authentication, and for enabling of encryption.

The LMP PDUs are transferred in the payload instead of ordinary data. They are always sent as single-slot packets and they can be carried in two different types of data packets. In order to distinguish LMP packets from other packets, a special type code is used in the packet header of all LMP messages. To avoid overflow in the receiving packet buffer, flow control is normally applied to the asynchronous data packet in Bluetooth. However, no flow control applies to LMP PDUs. The LMP PDU payload format is shown in Figure 1.4. The

Table 1.2

Summary of Synchronous Packets and Their Achievable Data Rates (in Kbps)

Type	Payload (Information Bytes)	FEC	CRC	Symmetric Max. Rate
HV1	10	1/3	No	64
HV2	20	2/3	No	64
HV3	30	No	No	64
DV	$10 + (0–9)^*$	$2/3^*$	Yes^*	$64 + 57.6^*$
EV3	1–30	No	Yes	96
EV4	1–120	2/3	Yes	192
EV5	1–180	No	Yes	288

*Marked items of the DV packet are only relevant to the data part of the payload.

PDU format can be considered as one byte header followed by the LM data. The header has two fields. The first field is only 1 bit long and contains the transaction *identifier* (ID). The second field is 7 bits long and contains the *operation code* (OpCode). The operation code tells which type of LMP PDU that is being sent. Each LMP message has its unique OpCode.

As we have described, the LMP is used to control and set up the link. A typical PDU flow example at connection creation is shown in Figure 1.5. The connection establishment always starts with the master unit paging the slave unit. After the basic baseband page and page response messages have been exchanged, the setup of the link can start. Before the master sends a connection request, it might request information from the slave regarding its clock, version of the link manager protocol, LMP features, and the name of the slave units. A set of LMP PDUs has been defined for this purpose. The connection setup procedure then really starts with the master sending the **LMP connection request** message. Next, the security-related message exchange takes place. Finally, the peers complete the connection setup by exchanging **LMP setup complete** messages. Special security related PDUs have been defined in order to accomplish:

- Pairing;
- Authentication;
- Encryption;
- Changing the link key.

The details of principles and usage are described in Chapters 2 and 3. In addition to the different LM functions we have mentioned previously, the LM is also responsible for performing role change (master-slave switch), controlling multislot packet size, and power control.

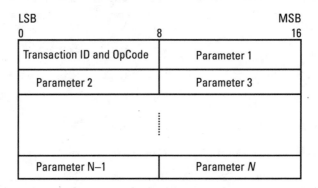

Figure 1.4 The LMP PDU format.

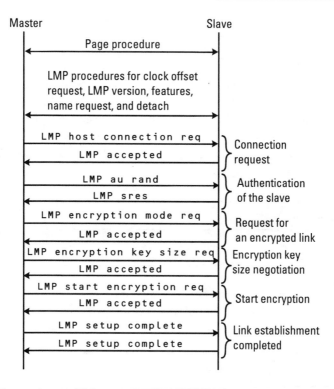

Figure 1.5 Connection establishment example, LMP PDU flow.

1.1.7 Logical link control and adaptation protocol

The L2CAP takes care of datagram segmentation and reassembly, multiplexing of service streams, and quality-of-service issues. The L2CAP constitutes a filter between the Bluetooth independent higher layers running on the host and the lower layers belonging to the Bluetooth module. For instance, *transmission control protocol/internet protocol* (TCP/IP) traffic packets are too large to fit within a baseband packet. Therefore, such packets will be cut into smaller chunks of data before they are sent to the baseband for further processing. On the receiving side, the process is reversed; baseband packets are reassembled into larger entities before being released to higher layers.

1.1.8 Host control interface

The HCI is a common standardized interface between the upper and lower layers in the Bluetooth communication stack. As we described in Section 1.1.3, the HCI provides the capability of separating the radio hardware-related functions from higher layer protocols, which might run on a separate host processor. By using the HCI, it is possible to use one Bluetooth module for several different hosts and applications. Similar, upper-layer applications implemented in one host can use any Bluetooth module supporting the HCI.

Figure 1.6 provides an overview of the lower Bluetooth layers and the HCI interface. The HCI commands for the Bluetooth module are handled by the HCI firmware that access the baseband and link manager.

Not all Bluetooth implementations run the lower and higher layer processing on different processors. Integrated implementations are also possible. Consequently, the HCI is an optional feature and only products that benefit from the separation use it.

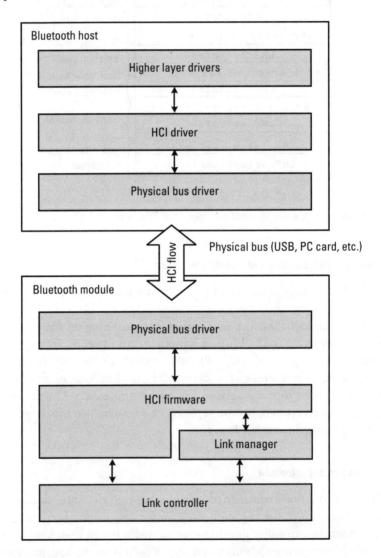

Figure 1.6 Overview of the lower software layers and the position of the HCI stack.

The HCI commands are transported between the Bluetooth module and host by some physical bus. This can, for example, be a *universal serial bus* (USB) or PC card connection. Three physical transport media have been defined [4]: USB, RS232, and universal asynchronous receiver/transmitter (UART). The host exchanges data with the module by using *command packets,* and the module gives responses to these requests or sends its own commands to the host, which are called *event packets.* Data to be passed over a Bluetooth link is transported in *data packets.*

To prevent buffer overflow in the host controller, flow control is used in the direction from the host to the host controller. The host keeps track of the size of the buffer all the time. At initialization, the host issues the `Read Buffer Size` command. The host controller then continuously informs the host of the number of completed transmitted packets through the `Number of Completed Packet` event.

The command packets can be divided into six different subgroups:

1. Link control commands;
2. Link policy commands;
3. Host controller and baseband commands;
4. Read information commands;
5. Read status commands;
6. Test commands.

The link control commands are used to control the link layer connections to other Bluetooth devices. Control of authentication and encryption as well as keys and pass-key commands belong to this subgroup. The policy commands are used to control how the link manager manages the piconet. The host controller and baseband commands are used to read and write into several different host controller registers. This includes reading and writing keys and pass-keys to or from the host controller, as well as reading and writing the general link manager authentication and encryption policy (see Section 2.5). The read information commands are used to get information about the Bluetooth device and the capabilities of the host controller. Information on connection states and signal strength can be obtained through the read status commands. Finally, the test commands are used to test various functionalities of the Bluetooth hardware.

1.1.9 Profiles

The Bluetooth standard is not limited to specific use cases or applications. However, in order to offer interoperability and to provide support for specific applications, the Bluetooth SIG has developed a set of so-called *profiles.* A profile defines an unambiguous description of the communication interface between two units for one particular service. Both basic profiles that define fundamental procedures for Bluetooth connections and profiles for distinct services have been defined.

A new profile can be built on existing ones, allowing efficient reuse of existing protocols and procedures. This gives raise to a hierarchical profiles structure as outlined in Figure 1.7. The most fundamental definitions, recommendations, and requirements related to modes of operation and connection and channel setup are given in the *generic access profile* (GAP). All other existing Bluetooth profiles make use of the GAP. The very original purpose of the Bluetooth standard was short-range cable replacement. Pure cable replacement through RS232 emulation is offered by the *serial port profile*. Several other profiles, like the *personal area network* (PAN) and *local positioning profile* make use

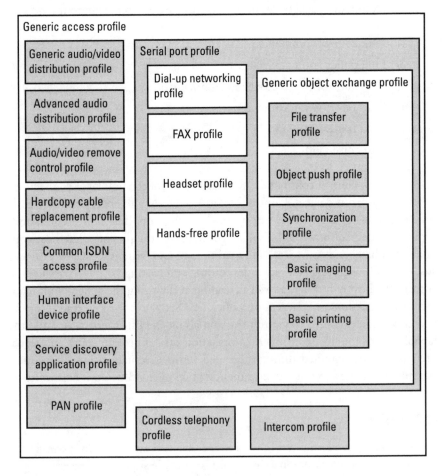

Figure 1.7 Bluetooth profiles.

of the *serial port profile*. One level deeper in the profiles hierarchy is the *general object exchange profile*. The purpose of this profile is to describe how the IrDA *object exchange* (OBEX) layer is used within Bluetooth. OBEX can be used to any higher layer object exchange, such as synchronization, file transfer, and push services.

Different services have different security requirements. In Section 10 we discuss the security requirements and solutions for a selection of Bluetooth profiles. Most profiles benefit from using the baseband security functions. It is important, though, that the mechanisms are correctly understood and that application providers are aware of the strength as well as limitations of the link level security services. New profiles are constantly being developed, and some existing profiles may become replaced as others covering the same or similar functionality are added. Profiles are released independently of the core specification release schedule. In Figure 1.7 we have included the profiles that were adopted at the time of this writing (November 2003).

1.2 Bluetooth security basics

Security issues surfaced from the beginning in the design of the Bluetooth system. It was decided that even for the simplest usage scenarios, the Bluetooth system should provide security features. To find the correct level of security when a new communication technology is defined is a nontrivial task, as it depends on usage. Bluetooth is versatile, which further increases the difficulties in finding the correct level one anticipates for the system. We start this section by discussing some typical user scenarios for Bluetooth applications.

1.2.1 User scenarios

In Section 1.1.9 we touched upon Bluetooth profiles. The overview of the profiles shows that the technology can be used in a large number of different applications. The overview also demonstrates that very different devices with very different capabilities might utilize the local connectivity provided by Bluetooth. However, most applications are characterized by two things: *personal area usage* and *ad hoc connectivity*. The Bluetooth link level security mechanisms have been designed with these two characteristics in mind, and below we describe what we mean by personal area networks and ad hoc connectivity.

Personal area networks

The personal area network concept is a vision shared among a large number of researchers and wireless technology drivers. A PAN consists of a limited number of units that have the ability to form networks and exchange information. The units can be under one user's control (i.e., personal computing units) or they can be controlled by different users or organizations. Bluetooth is used as a local connection interface between different personal units, such as mobile phones, laptops, *personal digital assistants* (PDA), printers, keyboards, mouses, headsets, and loudspeakers. Hence, Bluetooth is a true enabling technology for the PAN vision. The devices are typically (but not at all limited to) consumer devices. Different consumer devices have different manufacturers, and the personal usage of a device will vary from person to person. Hence, in order to provide interoperability between the different personal devices, the security must to some extent be configured by the user. Bluetooth security solutions have been designed with the principles in mind that any ordinary user should be able to configure and manage the necessary security actions needed to protect the communication links.

The information exchanged over Bluetooth might very well be sensitive and vulnerable to eavesdropping. In addition, users of mobile phones or laptops would like to be sure that no unauthorized (by the users) person is able to connect to their personal devices. Another issue is location privacy. People would like to use their Bluetooth devices anywhere they go without fearing that somebody can track their movements. To ensure that, device anonymity is an important user expectation.

To sum up, there are four fundamental security expectations for Bluetooth:

1. Easy-to-use and self-explanatory security configuration;
2. Confidentiality protection;
3. Authentication of connecting devices;
4. Anonymity.

Bluetooth provides link encryption and authentication. In this book we will provide a possible solution for providing anonymity (see Chapter 8). If the expectation for easy-to-use and self-explanatory security configuration has also been fulfilled is hard to say—at least the system has been designed with this goal in mind.

Ad hoc connectivity

As discussed previously, Bluetooth has been designed to support the wireless PAN vision. Sometimes the relations between the devices are fixed, like the connection between a desktop computer and the keyboard or the mouse. Another example is the connection between a mobile phone and a headset. However, sometimes one wishes to set up connections on the fly with another device that just happens to be nearby. This is ad hoc connectivity. To illustrate an ad hoc connectivity scenario, we give an example. Let us consider a business meeting where two persons, an employee and a visitor, meet in a room equipped with a video projector, illustrated in Figure 1.8.

The two persons in the room are each carrying one laptop. The laptops contain presentation information that the users would like to present to each other using the video projector. Furthermore, after the presentation, the visitor would like to send a presentation to the employee. We assume that the video projector and the laptops support Bluetooth for local connectivity. Hence, we have a PAN scenario with three different Bluetooth-enabled devices:

1. A video projector;

2. A visitor laptop;

3. An employee laptop.

The ad hoc nature of these connections stems from the fact that no prior relation can be assumed between the visitor's laptop and the projector or between the visitor and employee laptop. Hence, in order to provide security (authentication and encryption) on the communication links, the security relations must be set up on the fly and often by the users themselves. The original Bluetooth pairing mechanism provides the possibility of setting up ad hoc security relations. However, one would like to minimize the load on the user and

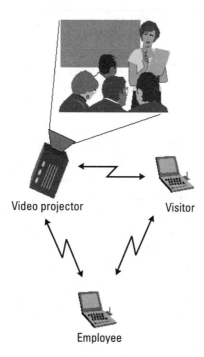

Video projector   Visitor

Employee

Figure 1.8 Bluetooth meeting room ad hoc connectivity scenario.

find alternative methods to manual procedures. In this book we revisit these issues several times and discuss features needed to make ad hoc connectivity as secure and, at the same time, as user friendly as possible. In the next chapter we will give an overview of the Bluetooth security architecture. But first we review some frequently used notions and terminology.

1.2.2   Notions and terminology

We already mentioned that security expectations for Bluetooth are related to the following four aspects (1) easy-to-use and self-explanatory security configuration, (2) confidentiality protection, (3) authentication of connecting devices, and (4) anonymity. These aspects describe what we mean by security in this book. When considering general information systems, security is understood to encompass the following three aspects [5]: confidentiality, integrity, and availability. The mechanisms that address the confidentiality aspects should provide the means to keep user information private. Integrity mechanisms address the capability to protect the data against unauthorized alterations or removal. Finally, availability deals with the aspect that the system should be available as expected. Availability is therefore closely related to reliability and robustness. Comparing this with what we said within the context of Bluetooth, we see that the aspects of confidentiality and availability appear in the four security expectations, although it may be argued that anonymity is an aspect on its own. The Bluetooth standard does not currently include any data integrity protection mechanism. In the sections that follow, we discuss first the meaning of confidentiality and integrity in more detail. We then continue to give a very compact description of cryptographic mechanisms that are used to achieve security.

Confidentiality

Confidentiality of data can be achieved by transforming the original data, often called the *plaintext*, into a new text, the *ciphertext*, that does not reveal the content of the plaintext. The transformation should be (conditionally) reversible, allowing the recovery of the plaintext from the ciphertext. To avoid that the transformation itself has to be kept secret to prevent a recovery of the plaintext, the transformation is realized as a parameterized transformation, where only the controlling parameter is kept secret. The controlling parameter is called the *key* and the transformation is called *encryption*. A good encryption mechanism has the property that unless the key value is known, it is practically infeasible to recover the plaintext or the key value from the ciphertext. What actually "practically infeasible" means is not exactly defined. Moreover, what is infeasible today may be feasible tomorrow. A good measure of the quality of an encryption mechanism is that even if very many plaintext and corresponding ciphertext messages are known, the amount of work to break a cipher (e.g., recover the key) is in the same order as the number of key combinations. In other words, breaking the cipher is equivalent to a complete search through the key space.

Integrity

The second aspect of security, that is, integrity, is about ensuring that data has not been replaced or modified without authorization during transport or storage. Integrity should not be confused with peer authentication or identification (see the explanation below), which can be used to verify the communication peer during connection setup. Peer authentication only guarantees that a connection is established with the supposed peer, while message integrity is about authenticity of the transmitted messages. Integrity protection of transmitted data is not part of the Bluetooth standard.

Symmetric and asymmetric mechanisms

Cryptographic mechanisms are distinguished as being either *symmetric key* or *asymmetric key*. Symmetric mechanisms are mechanisms for which the communicating parties share the same secret key. There is, so to speak, a symmetric situation among the parties. If the mechanism concerns the encryption of files, say, then the receiver is not only able to decrypt the files received from the transmitter, but in fact the receiver is able to decrypt encrypted files that were generated by the receiver itself. Thus, a receiver cannot claim that the decrypted data indeed was sent by the sender. Symmetric mechanisms (we sometimes also use the word *schemes*) are also called *secret-key mechanisms*. An important property of symmetric mechanisms is that the transportation of the key from the sending to the receiving party needs to be realized in such a way that no information about the key is leaked to outsiders. This need for key transfer constitutes the core problem in key management. Encryption of large data blocks is often realized through symmetric encryption mechanisms because they are faster than the asymmetric mechanisms. Secret-key mechanisms have a long history, and many variants are known and in use. The main two types of secret-key mechanisms are block and stream ciphers.

Asymmetric mechanisms are mechanisms that realize an encryption and decryption transformation pair for which the keys for the respective transformations are not the same. In fact, one demands that one of the keys cannot be recovered from the other. Hence, the keys at the sending and receiving sides have an asymmetry in their properties. Asymmetric mechanisms are also called *public-key mechanisms*. This naming stems from the fact that for asymmetric mechanism, one speaks about a private- and public-key pair. The private key is kept secret from everyone else and the public key is made accessible to everybody (i.e., it is made public). Asymmetric mechanisms solve some of the key distribution problems that arise in the activation of symmetric mechanisms. This advantage of asymmetric mechanisms is, however, often spoiled by the need to have proofs of the binding between a public key and an entity who claims to be the owner (of the private key). A widespread solution to this is the use of so-called *certificates*. Such certificates bind a public key to an identity[2] and are issued by a common trusted agent.

Public-key schemes are asymmetric cryptographic mechanisms. The two keys that relate to a pair of encryption and decryption transformations are called the public key and private key, respectively. Together they form a public- and private-key pair. In public-key schemes, the private key cannot be recovered by practical means from the public key or any other publicly known information for that matter.

The best known public-key schemes are the Rivest, Shamir, and Adleman (RSA) and Diffie-Hellman schemes. Both date back to the beginning of public-key cryptography in the 1970s. Diffie-Hellman is used for key establishment, while RSA is for key transport, encryption, or digital signatures. For more information and a historical overview, see [6].

Block and stream ciphers

Block ciphers are symmetric cryptographic mechanisms that transform a fixed amount of plaintext data (a block) to a block of ciphertext data using a key, and that have an inverse transformation using the same key (as used for the encryption transformation). See Figure 1.9(a). Block ciphers are very useful as building blocks to obtain other cryptographic mechanisms, such as authentication mechanisms. In Bluetooth, the SAFER+ block cipher is used in this manner, as will be described in Section 4.2.

Stream ciphers are the other main type of symmetric cryptographic mechanisms. Here a stream (sequence) of plaintext symbols is transformed symbol by symbol in a sequence of ciphertext symbols by adding, symbol by symbol, a so-called *key stream* to the sequence of plaintext symbols. See Figure 1.9(b). Stream ciphers have a trivial inverse transformation. Just generate the same key stream and subtract its symbols from the stream of cipher symbols. Bluetooth uses the E_0 stream cipher to encrypt the data sent via the radio links.

Authentication

Authentication is the procedure by which a unit (the verifier) can convince itself about the (correct) identity of another unit (the claimant) it is communicating with[3]. Note that in cryptography, one often refers to this as the *identification*, and authentication is reserved for referring to (message or data) authenticity,

---

2. This is the most common use of certificates. However, there are types of certificates other than identity certificates, and certificates often carry other information as well, often telling about limitations of the use of the key (pair).

3. In [5] this is called peer authentication.

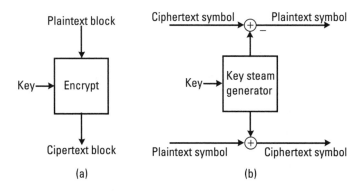

Figure 1.9 (a) Block cipher, and (b) stream cipher.

that is, the problem of asserting that a received message is authentic (as sent by the sender). Here we use the definition of authentication that is in use in many (cellular) communication systems [e.g., Global Mobile System (GSM) and wideband code division multiple access (WCDMA)], that is, it refers to the process of verifying the consistency of the link keys in the involved Bluetooth devices exchanged during the pairing procedure.

Authorization

Authorization is the process of giving someone permission to do or have access to something. For Bluetooth this means to decide whether a remote device has the right to access a service on the local host and what privileges to gain for it. Usually this involves some form of user interaction. Alternatively, granting access to services can be subject to device-specific settings. Sometimes authorization refers both to administering system permission settings and the actual checking of the permission values when a device is getting access.

References

[1]   Bluetooth Special Interest Group, *Specification of the Bluetooth System, Version 1.2, Core System Package,* November 2003.

[2]   Bluetooth Special Interest Group, *Specification of the Bluetooth System, Version 1.2, Core System Package, Part B, Baseband Specification, Link Controller Operation,* November 2003.

[3]   Lin, S., and D. J. Costello Jr., *Error Control Coding: Fundamentals and Applications,* Englewood Cliffs, NJ: Prentice-Hall, Inc., 1983.

[4]   Bluetooth Special Interest Group, *Specification of the Bluetooth System, Version 1.2, Core System Package, Part E, Host Controller Interface Functional Specification,* November 2003.

[5]   CCITT: International Telegraph and Telephone Consultative Committee, *X.800: Data Communication Networks: Open Systems Interconnection (OSI); Security, Structure and Applications*, International Telecommunication Union, Geneva, 1991.

[6]   van Oorschot, P.C., A. J. Menezes, and S. A. Vanstone, *Handbook of Applied Cryptography*, Boca Raton, FL: CRC Press, 1997.

2

Overview of the Bluetooth Security Architecture

The security demands in the various usage scenarios for Bluetooth differ substantially. For example, a remote-controlled toy and a remote-controlled industrial robot constitute usage cases with essentially different demands on security. The security architecture for Bluetooth is designed to provide built-in security features even for the simplest cases and at the same time provide adequate support to provide security in demanding cases, such as those where Bluetooth devices are used in a network environment.

This chapter gives an overview of the Bluetooth security architecture, starting with a description of the different key types that are used, how the link encryption is organized, and how all the basic features are controlled through security modes to achieve different trust relations.

2.1 Key types

The security provided by the Bluetooth core is built upon the use of symmetric-key cryptographic mechanisms for authentication, link encryption, and key generation. A number of different key types are used in connection with these mechanisms. In Bluetooth, a link is a communication channel that is established between two Bluetooth devices. To check that a link is established between the correct devices, an authentication procedure between two devices has been introduced. The authentication mechanism in this procedure uses the so-called *link key*. As we will find out later, there are several different types of link keys. Link keys are not only used for authentication. They are also used for derivation of the key that controls the encryption of the data sent via a link. Through this encryption, confidentiality of the transmitted data is realized. The corresponding encryption mechanism uses the *link encryption key*. Loosely speaking, a link key is used for the authentication between two devices and to derive the link encryption key. A link key is created during the pairing of two devices. Section 2.2 contains more details on the pairing and use of pass-keys.

Before we discuss the pairing mechanism, it is useful to clarify the conditions under which communication between two devices will occur. It is important to distinguish two important states. Firstly, we have the state in which a device wants to establish a connection with a device it has not been paired with. Secondly, we have the state where a device wants to communicate with a device it has paired with. Of course, a device may, as a result of a malfunction or a forced reset, have lost the pairing information associated with a device. In such a situation, the device should fall back to the unpaired state.

The pairing operation will result in a link key that two devices will use for authentication and link encryption key generation directly after the pairing and at later instances. The Bluetooth system recognizes two types of link keys: *semipermanent* and *temporary keys*. Furthermore, two types of semipermanent (link) keys are distinguished: *unit keys* and *combination keys*. A unit key is a link key that one unit generates by itself and uses as a link key with any other (Bluetooth) device, and a combination key is a key that a device generates in cooperation (combination) with another device. Therefore, any unit key that a specific device has may be known to many other devices, whereas each combination key is only known to itself and the device with which it was generated. Unit keys can only be safely used when there is full trust among the devices that are paired with the same unit key. This is because every paired device can impersonate any other device holding the same unit key. Since Bluetooth version 1.2, the use of unit keys is not recommended. But, for legacy reasons, unit keys have not been completely removed from the specification. Besides the combination and unit keys, two other key types are used: *initialization keys* and *master keys*. These are temporary keys. The initialization key is a short-lived key that exists during the pairing of two devices. The master key is a link key that the master generates prior to the setup of an encrypted broadcast communication to several slave devices. Besides the link keys, we have three ciphering keys: *the encryption key K_C*, the *constrained encryption key K'_C*, and the *payload key K_P*. The encryption key is the main key that controls the ciphering. Since this key may have a length (in bits) that exceeds legislative constraints on the maximally allowed key length, K_C is not used directly but is replaced by the constrained encryption key K'_C, whose number of independent bits can be selected from 8, 16, . . . , 128 bits. Currently there is little reason to accept key lengths less than 128 bits because the export regulations have been relaxed since the original design of the Bluetooth system. It is directly derived from K_C. Finally, the payload key is a ciphering key derived from the constrained encryption key K'_C. This key is the initial state of the ciphering engine prior to generating the overlay sequence. A summary of the different key types can be found in Table 2.1. More details on the encryption keys is given in Section 2.4.1.

2.2 Pairing and user interaction

As indicated earlier, the pairing of two devices is the procedure by which two devices establish a shared secret that they can use when they meet again. The pairing requires user interaction, for example, the entering of a pass-key.[1] See Figure 2.1(a). The Bluetooth system allows the pass-key to be 128 bits long. Such a large pass-key value would be rather user unfriendly for manual input. However, this feature allows the use of a higher level automated key agreement scheme that can "feed" the agreed pass-key into the pairing procedure. See Figure 2.1(b). The high-level key agreement scheme can be a network or *transport layer security* (TLS) protocol. Examples of such protocols are the Internet Engineering Task Force (IETF) protocols TLS [1] and Internet key exchange (IKE) [2].

There are two kinds of pass-keys in Bluetooth terminology: the *variable* pass-key and the *fixed* pass-key. The first type represents a pass-key that can be arbitrarily chosen at the pairing instance. This requires that some form of user interaction takes place in order to feed the Bluetooth device with the appropriate pass-key value. This interaction is most likely accomplished using a keyboard or numerical keypad. An example of a typical device with a variable pass-key is the mobile phone. In contrast, the fixed pass-key cannot be chosen arbitrarily when it is needed. Instead, a predetermined value must be used. This type of pass-key is used when there is no user interface to input a value to the Bluetooth

Table 2.1
Overview of Key Types

Purpose	Semipermanent		Temporary	
Authentication key generation	Unit key	Combination key	Initialization key	Master key
Ciphering			Encryption key Constrained encryption key	Payload key

---

1. In the Bluetooth specification, one sometimes uses the term personal identification number (PIN).

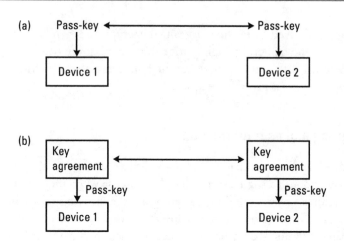

Figure 2.1 (a) Pairing through manual user interaction, and (b) pairing through separate key
agreement protocol.

device. Clearly, for a pairing to work, only one device can have a fixed pass-key
(unless, of course, both devices happen to have the same fixed pass-key). Examples of devices in need of fixed pass-keys are Bluetooth-enabled mice and headsets. These gadgets come with a factory preset pass-key when delivered to the
customer.

Note that a fixed pass-key need not be "fixed" in the sense that it can never
be changed. Preferably, the user is allowed to change the fixed pass- key in some
way. In some scenarios, a wired connection could be used, for example, by plug-
ging in an external keyboard and changing the pass-key. This is only feasible if it
is difficult for anyone but the rightful owner to have physical access to the Bluetooth device in question. More interesting is to allow the change over Bluetooth
using an already paired device (equipped with the necessary user interface) over
a *secure connection*. This implies that the user connects to the device with a fixed
pass-key, authenticates itself, and requests the link to be encrypted before a fresh
pass-key value can be sent to the remote device. The new value replaces the old
one and becomes the fixed pass-key to use in subsequent pairings. In Chapter 3
we will come back to the details of the pairing procedure.

2.3 Authentication

A Bluetooth device in a connectable state accepts connection requests from
other devices. This means that there is a risk that a connectable device is connected to and attacked by a malicious device. Obvious, this can be avoided by
never entering a connectable state. On the other hand, that implies that no
Bluetooth connections at all can be established. Accordingly, there is a need to

securely identify the other communication peer so that connections from unknown devices can be refused. Device identification is provided through the Bluetooth authentication mechanism. The authentication procedure is a so-called challenge-response scheme, where the *verifier* device sends a random challenge to the *claimant* device and expects a valid response value in return. The authentication procedure is only one way, and if mutual authentication is needed the procedure must be repeated with the verifier and claimant roles switched. In Section 3.4.4 the authentication procedure is described in more detail.

2.4 Link privacy

Of all security aspects encountered in wireless scenarios, the easiest to understand is the one relating to confidentiality. Eavesdropping on a radio transmission can be accomplished without revealing anything to the victim. Radio waves are omnidirectional and travel through walls (at least to some extent). One can easily imagine hiding a small radio receiver close enough to intercept the messages sent by a user, without revealing its presence to anyone not knowing where to look for it. It may even be possible to do this without having physical access to the premises where the Bluetooth devices are used. If the walls surrounding the user area are not completely shielding the radio transmissions, eavesdropping can take place outside this room.

Initially, Bluetooth was envisioned as a simple cable replacement technology. For some applications (such as device synchronization), replacing the wire with a radio has implications for confidentiality. It was desirable that the user should not experience any decrease in confidentiality when comparing the wireless with the wired solution. Thus, it was determined to look into what kind of security means were needed in order to give a sufficient degree of protection to Bluetooth communication.

In contrast to what sometimes has been claimed, the frequency hopping scheme used in Bluetooth gives no real protection against eavesdropping. Firstly, there is no secret involved in generating the sequence of visited channels—it is determined by the master's LAP and native clock. Clearly, these two variables are not secret. Adversaries may have full knowledge of them by following the inquiry/page procedure traffic preceding the connection that they are now eavesdropping on. Alternatively, adversaries can simply connect to the master to automatically get all necessary information. Secondly, there are only 79 channels used. By running this many receivers in parallel (one for each channel) and recording all traffic, an offline attack seems feasible simply by overlaying all 79 recordings.

2.4.1 Protect the link

It is important to understand that Bluetooth specifies security for the link between radio units, not for the entire path from source to destination at the application layer. All protocols and profiles that need end-to-end protection will have to provide for this themselves. The implications are obvious in access point scenarios, where the remote application may be running on a unit located thousands of kilometers away, and traffic routing will involve many unknown links apart from the short radio link between the local unit and the access point. Since the user has no control over this, higher layer security is an understandable prerequisite to ensuring confidentiality all the way. However, even in the case when the source and destination reside on PDAs close to each other and there is only one direct Bluetooth link in between, one should remember that Bluetooth security only addresses the radio link. Who is really in control on the other side? Can malicious software access and control the Bluetooth radio?

2.4.2 Encryption algorithm

When it comes to the selection of which encryption algorithm to use, there are some considerations that need to be taken into account:

- Algorithmic complexity;
- Implementation complexity;
- Strength of the cipher.

Algorithmic complexity relates to the number of computations needed for encryption and decryption, while implementation complexity relates to the size of the implementation on silicon. These two items boil down to power consumption and cost—crucial properties for the battery-powered units Bluetooth is designed for. A complex algorithm will almost certainly require a larger footprint on silicon than does a simple algorithm, leading to higher cost. For the implementation, sometimes the speed obtained from dedicated hardware can be traded for flexibility and smaller size using a programmable component such as a *digital signal processor* (DSP) or a small *central processing unit* (CPU). For such solutions, an increased algorithmic complexity will inevitably demand higher clocking frequency, which also increases power consumption.

The last item on the list may be the most important. Should the ciphering algorithm prove to be vulnerable to some "simple" attack, the whole foundation of link privacy falls. Of course, the question of whether an attack is "simple" or not remains to be discussed, but, in general, even the smallest suspicion regarding strength is enough to cast doubts over the system's overall security quality. Do not confuse algorithmic complexity of encryption/decryption with the strength of the cipher. In fact, the goal is to keep the algorithmic complexity low while having the computational complexity for all types of attacks as high as possible.

Bluetooth deploys a stream cipher (see Section 1.2.2) with the desired properties of a small and simple hardware solution while being difficult to break. A key stream is added modulo 2 to the information sequence. Thus, the scheme is symmetric, since the same key is used for encryption and decryption. This means the same hardware can be used for encryption and decryption, something that will actively keep down the size of the implementation. Moreover, stream ciphers are built efficiently using *linear feedback shift registers* (LFSR), which helps to reduce the die size even further.

The encryption/decryption consists of three identifiable parts: initialization of a payload key, generating the key stream bits, and, finally, the actual process of encrypting and decrypting the data. These functions are depicted in Figure 2.2. The payload key is generated out of different input bits that are "randomized" by running the sequence generating circuitry of the key stream generator for a while. Then the payload key is used as the starting state for the key stream generator in the encryption process. Since the sequence generating circuitry is used also for generating the payload key, the implementation is mainly concentrated in this part. The last part simply consists of XORing[2] the key stream bits with the outgoing data stream (for encryption) or the demodulated received sequence (for decryption). The details for all this can be found in Section 4.3.

The choice of a stream cipher was to a large extent based on implementation considerations. Clearly, a key stream generator needs to fulfill a whole range of properties to make it useful for cryptographic purposes. For instance, the

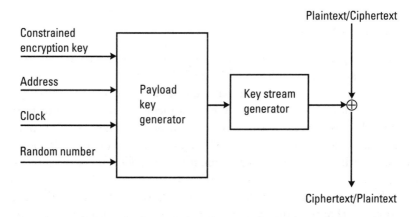

Figure 2.2 Stream cipher usage in Bluetooth. Encryption and decryption use the same circuitry.

---

2. Addition modulo 2.

sequence must have a large period and a high linear complexity, and satisfy standard statistical and cryptographic tests. A more thorough discussion about this can be found in Section 4.1.2.

As can be seen in Figure 2.2, there are some parameters involved in creating the payload key, K_P. The secret constrained encryption key, K'_C, is generated by both units at the time a decision is made to switch encryption on. This key is fixed for the duration of the session or until a decision is made to use a temporary key (which will require a change of the encryption key). Even though the constrained encryption key always consists of 128 bits, its true entropy will vary between 8 and 128 bits (in steps of 8 bits), depending on the outcome of the link key negotiation that the involved units must perform before encryption can be started. The *address* refers to the 48-bit Bluetooth unit address of the master, while the *clock* is 26 bits from the master's native clock. Finally, there is a 128-bit *random number* that is changed every time the encryption key is changed. This number is issued by the master before entering encryption mode and it is sent in plaintext over the air. The purpose of it is to introduce more variance into the generated payload key.

In Bluetooth, the key stream bits are generated by a method derived from the summation stream cipher generator in Massey and Rueppel [3]. This method is well investigated, and good estimates of its strength with respect to currently known methods for cryptanalysis exist. The summation generator is known to have some weaknesses that can be utilized in correlation attacks, but, thanks to the high resynchronization frequency (see Section 2.4.3) of the generator, these attacks will not be practical threats to Bluetooth. In Section 7.1 this will be discussed in greater detail.

2.4.3   Mode of operation

Not all bits of a Bluetooth packet are encrypted. The access code, consisting of a preamble, sync word, and a trailer, must be readable to all units in order for them to succeed in their receiver acquisition phase (i.e., in locking onto the radio signal). Furthermore, all units of a piconet must be able to read the packet header to see if the message is for them or not. Therefore, it is only the payload that is encrypted. The ciphering takes place after the CRC is added but before the optional error correcting code is applied. The principle is illustrated in Figure 2.3.

In generating the payload key, bits 1 to 26 of the master clock are used. This implies a change of the resulting key for every slot, since bit 1 toggles every 625 μs. However, the payload key is only generated at the start of a packet; multislot packets will not require a change of the payload key when passing a slot boundary within the packet. Consequently, for every Bluetooth baseband payload, the key stream generator will be initialized with a different starting

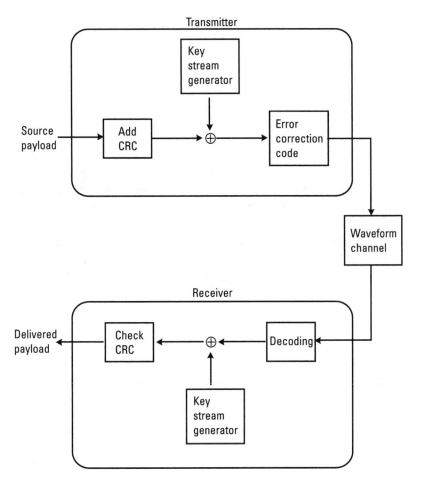

Figure 2.3 How to format encrypted packets.

state. This frequent change of the starting state is a key factor in its resistance to correlation attacks.

The initialization phase takes some time. In principle, the input parameters are loaded into the shift registers of the key stream generator, which is then run to produce 200 output bits. Of these, the last 128 are retained and subsequently reloaded into the shift registers. These operations put a limit to how fast one can change from one payload key to another. Fortunately, Bluetooth specifies a guard space between the end of a payload and the start of the next of at least[3] 259 μs. The guard space is there in order to allow for the frequency synthesizer of the radio to stabilize at the next channel used before the start of the

---

3. The shortest guard space is for HV3 packets.

next packet. During this time (and, in principle, also during the $72 + 54\ \mu s$ of plaintext access code and packet header), the payload key initialization can be run without interfering with the encryption or decryption process. The principle is shown in Figure 2.4.

2.4.4 Unicast and broadcast

Broadcast encryption poses a slight problem due to the point-to-point paradigm used in Bluetooth. In principle, apart from itself, a slave device is only aware of the piconet master. Thus the slave has no security bonding to other slave members. Specifically, each link in the piconet uses different encryption keys, since they are all based on their respective link keys. If the master would like to send an encrypted message to all its slaves, it can do this using individually addressed messages (also known as *unicast messages*) which will introduce unnecessary overhead. A better alternative is for the master to change all link keys to a temporary key, the *master key*. Based on this, all devices are able to generate a common encryption key that can be used in broadcast transmissions that address all slaves simultaneously.

One drawback with this approach is that mixing secure unicast traffic and secure broadcast traffic is not possible. The user must settle for one of these at a time. The reason is in the packet structure and required initialization time for the payload key. A broadcast message is identified from the all-zero *LT_ADDR*, while unicast messages have nonzero *LT_ADDR*. This 3-bit address field is part of the payload header. Not until this information has been received and interpreted can the receiver decide whether the payload key should be based on the encryption key used for unicast or broadcast traffic. By then, there is far too little time (less than $48\ \mu s$) to generate the payload key before the packet payload is being received unless very fast hardware (i.e., involving high clock frequency) is used. This, however, would put unrealistic requirements on the ciphering hardware and increase cost as well as power consumption. It is, of course,

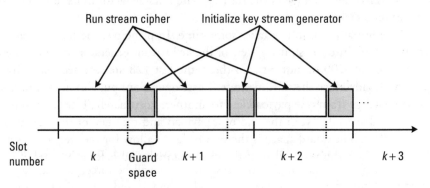

Figure 2.4 Operation of the encryption machinery.

inappropriate to use the broadcast encryption key for unicast traffic also, since all devices within the piconet are able to decipher this. Broadcast encryption will be discussed in Chapter 5.

2.5 Communication security policies

Security always comes at the prize of higher complexity. Hence, the security mechanisms should only be used when they are really needed. When and how to use the mechanisms is determined by the security policies of a device. The Bluetooth standard provides some basic principles for enforcing link-level security and building more advanced security polices through the three defined security modes.

One obvious choice for protecting Bluetooth communication is using the built-in link-level security mechanisms. Authentication and encryption is provided at baseband level. Using the built-in mechanisms has the advantage of protecting all layers above the link level (including control messages). The link-level security mechanisms can be switched on or off. The security policy determines if a device demands authentication and/or encryption. One very simple approach is to demand maximum link-level security, that is, both authentication and encryption for all connections. This is an "always-on" link-level security policy. Such a simple policy has several advantages. First, the complexity is low. Furthermore, it gives a high level of security for all local connections and it is easy to implement. Finally, it is easy for the user to handle and understand the security policy. This kind of always-on policy and security enforcement is supported by Bluetooth security mode 3 (see Section 2.5.1). In order for this policy to be user convenient, the necessary keys must be present. If one can assume or actually demand that this is the case, the simple, always-on policy can be used and the security mechanisms are very easy to handle. Obviously, this policy also has some drawbacks:

- If the necessary link keys are not present, either a connection cannot be established or the keys need to be generated and exchanged at connection creation.
- If the necessary link keys are not present and the key exchange cannot be done automatically, the users must be involved and they must understand what is happening.

The latter implication can be a serious drawback, when the actual service does not demand any security. In this case, the user will be forced to handle a security procedure for a service that may need to be fast and convenient. Some device might only run services with high security requirements, and consequently this will not cause any problem. On the other hand, devices used at public places for information retrieval or exchange will certainly not have high security requirements for all its connections, and people using such services will probably not accept any tedious security procedures. Hence, a policy that demands link-level security for some services and keeps some services totally "open" will be needed. In practice, this implies that a device will need a shared secret with some other device, and at the same time the device must be able to communicate with other devices without sharing any secrets and using link-level security.

In summary, the simple, always-on security policy is not sufficient for all Bluetooth usage scenarios. A better flexibility link-level security mechanism enforcement is necessary. This can be achieved by service level–enabled security (aligned with the access control mechanism). This is the motivation for the introduction of security mode 2 (see Section 2.5.1), which allows service level–enabled link layer security.

2.5.1   Security modes

The GAP [4] defines the generic procedure related to the discovery of Bluetooth devices and the link management aspects of connecting to Bluetooth devices. The GAP also defines the different basic security procedures of a Bluetooth device. A connectable device can operate in three different *security modes*:

- *Security mode 1:* A Bluetooth unit in security mode 1 never initiates any security procedures; that is, it never demands authentication or encryption of the Bluetooth link.

- *Security mode 2:* When a Bluetooth unit is operating in security mode 2, it shall not initiate any security procedures, that is, demand authentication or encryption of the Bluetooth link, at link establishment. Instead, security is enforced at channel (L2CAP) or connection (e.g., Service Discovery Protocol (SDP), RFCOMM, TCS) establishment.

- *Security mode 3:* When a Bluetooth unit is in security mode 3, it shall initiate security procedures before the link setup is completed. Two different security policies are possible: always demand authentication or always demand both authentication and encryption.

In the following sections we discuss the different modes and how they are used in Bluetooth applications.

Security mode 1

Security mode 1 is the "unsecured" mode in Bluetooth. A unit that offers its service to all connecting devices operates in security mode 1. This implies that the unit does not demand authentication or encryption at connection establishment. For example, an access point that offers information services to anybody is a possible usage scenario for security mode 1.

Supporting authentication is mandatory and a unit in security mode 1 must respond to any authentication challenge. However, the unit will never send an authentication challenge itself and mutual authentication is never performed. A unit in security mode 1 that does not support encryption will refuse any request for that. On the other hand, if encryption is supported, the unit should accept a request for switching encryption on.

Security mode 2

Security mode 2 has been defined in order to provide better flexibility in the use of Bluetooth link-level security. In security mode 2, no security procedures are initiated until a channel or connection request has been received. This means that it is up to the application or service to ask for security. Only when the application or service requires it will the authentication and/or encryption mechanisms be switched on. A sophisticated authentication and encryption policy based on the baseband mechanisms can be implemented using this principle. Security mechanisms enforcement and policy handling must be taken care of by the unit. One possibility is to use a "security manager" to handle this. In Section 2.5.2, we further discuss the role and implementation of a security manager.

Security mode 2 comes at the price of higher implementation complexity and the risk of faulty security policies that might compromise the security of the unit.

Security mode 3

In security mode 3, on the other hand, security procedures (authentication and/or encryption) are enforced at connection establishment. This is a simple, always-on security policy. The implementation is easy and that reduces the risks of any security implementation mistakes. The drawback is the lack of flexibility. The unit will not be generally accessible. All connecting units need to be authenticated.

Security modes and security mechanisms

The different security modes define how a unit will act at connection establishment. Independent of the current security mode, a unit shall respond to security requests in accordance with what is specified in the link manager protocol (see Section 1.1.6). Hence, a security mode only defines the security behavior of the unit, but the security level for a connection is determined by the security modes of both units. Let one of two units be in security mode 3 and consequently demand encryption. Then the connection will be encrypted if both units support encryption; otherwise the connection will be terminated.

Table 2.2 describes the different security mode options and the resulting security mechanisms, while in Figure 2.5 the channel establishment procedure for different security modes is illustrated. In the figure, the connection and service establishment procedure for a Bluetooth device is shown as a flow diagram. The process starts with the device that is in connectable mode. If the device is in security mode 3, it will try to authenticate and optionally encrypt the link directly after the link manager receives or makes a connection request. Specific host settings for access can be applied. For instance, devices that are not previously paired may be rejected. A device that is in security mode 1 or 2, on the other hand, will continue with the link setup procedure without any authentication or encryption request (see Chapter 6). Instead, the device in security mode 2 makes an access control check after a service connection has been requested. Access is only granted for authorized devices. Authorization is either given explicitly by the user or it can be given automatically (trusted and already paired device). For security mode 2, optional encryption can be requested before the connection to the service is finally established.

Service level access control can also be implemented by using security mode 3. Then authentication always takes place before the service request. Hence, security mode 2 gives better flexibility, since no security is enforced at

Table 2.2

The Different Security Mode Options for Master Respective Slave and Resulting Security Mechanism(s)

Slave Security Mode	Master Security Mode		
	1	2	3
1	No authentication, no encryption.	If the master application demands authentication (and encryption), then the link will be authenticated (and encrypted).	The link will be authenticated. If the master policy demands it, the link will be encrypted.
2	If the slave application demands it, the link will be authenticated (and encrypted).	If the master or slave application demands it, the link will be authenticated (and encrypted).	The link will be authenticated. If the master policy demands it, or if the slave application demands it, the link will be encrypted.
3	The link will be authenticated. If the slave policy demands it, the link will be encrypted.	The link will be authenticated. If the slave policy demands it, or the master application demands it, the link will be encrypted.	The link will be authenticated. If the slave or the master policy demands it, the link will be encrypted.

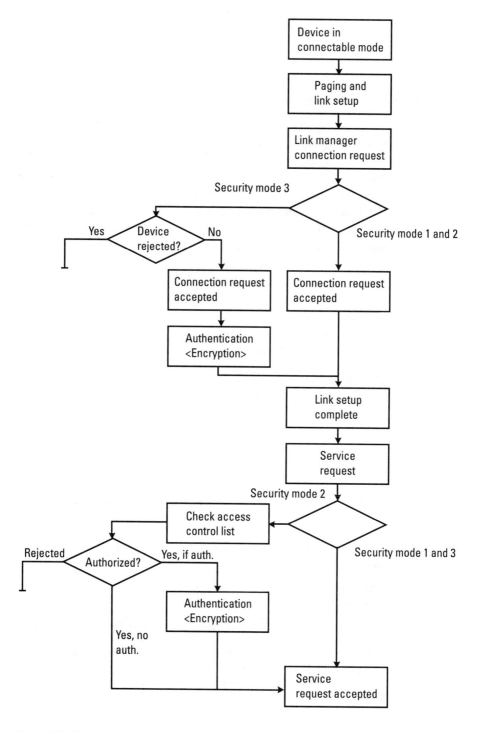

Figure 2.5 Channel establishment flow for different security modes.

channel or connection request. Thus it is possible to allow access to some services without any authentication or encryption and a unit can be totally open to some services while still restricting access to other services.

2.5.2 Security policy management

If security mode 2 is required together with a high security level, an advanced security policy must be implemented. One possibility is to use a security manager that handles the security policy and enforces the security mechanism. An example of how a security manager can be implemented in Bluetooth is given in [5]. According to these recommendations, the security manager is the responsible entity for security enforcement and it interacts with several different layers in the stack (see Section 1.1.3). In this architecture, an application or set of applications (referred to as *service*) register their security demands with the security manager. The security requirements of all supported applications make up the security policy. The security manager handles the policy. Since link-level security in Bluetooth is connected with the device address (through the link keys), the security manager needs access to a database, which contains information on different Bluetooth units, the corresponding link keys, and their level of trust. In addition to this, the manager needs access to a service database, which contains the specific security requirements of a particular service.

In Chapter 6 we describe how security policies can be managed in Bluetooth. We discuss different implementation alternatives and we also give a more detailed description of the recommendations given in [5].

References

[1]   Dierks, T., and C. Allen, *The TLS Protocol, Version 1.0, RFC 2246*, January 1999.

[2]   Harkins, D., and D. Carrel, *The Internet Key Exchange (IKE), RFC 2409*, November 1998.

[3]   Massey, J. L., and R. A. Rueppel, "Method of, and Apparatus for, Transforming a Digital Sequence into an Encoded Form," U.S. Patent No. 4,797,922, 1989.

[4]   Bluetooth Special Interest Group, *Specification of the Bluetooth System, Version 1.1, Profiles, Part K:1 Generic Access Profile*, February 2001.

[5]   Müller, T., ed., "Bluetooth Security Architecture," White Paper Revision 1.0, Bluetooth Special Interest Group, July 1999.

3

Bluetooth Pairing and Key Management

In this chapter we will have a closer look at pairing and key management in the Bluetooth system. Key management involves the generation, distribution, storage, and handling of the cryptographic keys. We recall from Table 2.1 that the main key types in Bluetooth are the link and encryption keys. Of these, the link key is the most important, since it is the basis for all future identifications between the units, and it is also used in the creation of an encryption key for each session requiring privacy. The link key is created during the pairing operation.

In the following sections we discuss pairing and Bluetooth key generation, storage, and updating of the link and encryption keys in more detail. We first give an overview of the pairing process as performed by Bluetooth 1.2 devices. We will show the involved steps and mechanisms in each of the Bluetooth stack layers.

3.1 Pairing in Bluetooth

The Bluetooth pairing operation is crucial in the process of establishing a secure connection (link) between two Bluetooth devices. To set up a Bluetooth connection, the involved procedure starts with establishing an ACL connection. When this task is completed, the Bluetooth devices can exchange messages on the radio channel. Before any user data can be exchanged, the devices can (optionally) require verification of their respective identities. In order to make use of the authentication and encryption mechanisms that provide protection against misuse and or wiretapping, the involved Bluetooth devices must establish some *shared secret*. It is during the pairing that this is accomplished.

The pairing procedure results in a bonding of two Bluetooth devices in the sense that after the pairing the devices share information that only the paired devices know. At this stage of connection setup, some user interaction is usually required in the form of entering a pass-key (compare Figure 2.1).

For convenience, Bluetooth devices must have the ability to store a number of (*link key, device address*) pairs in a database for later reference. Preferably, this information is stored in nonvolatile memory. Then when the Bluetooth devices meet again, they already have a link key and can skip the steps related to pairing. The exact number of such pairs is, of course, dependent on what type of application(s) the Bluetooth-enabled device runs. For PCs, the available memory resources should be more than enough to accommodate many hundreds of such pairs, while a phone headset with a very specific usage area need only save a few.

Even if pairing normally is only carried out for first-time connections, the pairing process is also automatically invoked if authentication is requested when one device for some reason (e.g., power failure or corruption of the link key database) has lost the link key for the connection.

The pairing procedure consists of the following steps:

- Generating an initialization key;
- Generating a link key;
- Link key exchange;
- Authentication.

How the pairing process is realized is explained in the following subsections for the HCI protocol, the LMP, and the baseband level, respectively.

3.2   HCI protocol

Using the *host controller and baseband commands*, it is possible to set the policy for authentication through the `Authentication Enable` command parameter. When this parameter is enabled, the local device will always authenticate the remote device at connection setup. Only if both units have this parameter disabled no authentication will take place. The setting of the parameter in the device depends on the current security mode. See Section 2.5.1.

Assuming the authentication is enabled in a device, the *host controller* (HC) will ask the host for a link key to use for the *BD_ADDR* of the remote device in the authentication protocol that is to be executed. This is, of course, unless the HC already has access to this key by itself (e.g., from caching or direct key storage access). If no such key can be found on the host, a negative response is sent back (`HCI Link Key Request Negative Reply`) over the HCI to the host controller. This "failure" event will initiate the pairing procedure.

The first thing needed in the pairing is a pass-key. The HC generates an `HCI PIN Code Request` event. The reply either consists of a pass-key (plus some additional information) or a negative response indicating that the host for some reason cannot specify a pass-key to use for the connection. The latter will ultimately cause the pairing request with the remote device to fail. When things work as intended, the HC at the initiating side can send the pass-key to the baseband for further processing. Next the LM will send a 128-bit random number (*IN_RAND*) to the remote device, which will trigger an `HCI PIN Code Request event` there as well.

From now on it is the LM that runs the pairing. The LMP ensures that a shared secret, the link key, is generated at both the local and remote devices. Depending on the device configuration, the link key can be a *unit key* or a *combination key*. The former is completely determined by one of the devices and the latter is constructed using contributions from both devices. Once the LMs have finished negotiating the link key, both hosts will be notified through the HCI Link Key Notification event.

3.3 LM protocol

The LM assists in the pairing procedure by communicating parameters and results between the local and remote devices. The calculations are done in the baseband. On the link manager level, the pairing procedure starts with the transmission of the PDU `LMP in rand` (containing the 128-bit random number *IN_RAND*) from one of the units to the other. This PDU will trigger the generation of the initialization key for use in the protocol for creating the actual link key.

If a unit key is to be used, the `LMP unit key` command is sent in one direction only, with the secret unit key XORed with the initialization key as its parameter. The receiver can easily calculate the key from this. See Section 3.4.2. If a combination key is to be created, two contributions (one from each side) are needed. This is accomplished through the `LMP comb key` PDU. The argument of this PDU is also a random number, but generating this and deriving the link key from it is slightly more complicated. For details, see Section 3.4.3.

After these PDUs have been exchanged, both ends are able to compute the link key. As a final check of success of this procedure and the established link key, a mutual authentication event is performed. A 128-bit challenge is sent through the `LMP au rand`, and the 32-bit response uses the `LMP sres` PDU. If neither of these authentications fails, both the local and the remote HCs notify their respective hosts.

It is important to stress the fact that the initialization key is used in only one pairing instance; afterward it is discarded.

3.4 Baseband events

At the baseband level, the LM protocol key management commands are turned into series of baseband events. The most important key management baseband events are those that support the pairing of two devices, the establishment of a link key, and the establishment of the ciphering offset and ciphering keys. Figure 3.1 gives an overview of the events.

As previously described, the LM initiates a pairing operation between two devices when the two devices meet the first time or a link key is missing due to other reasons. We recall from Table 2.1 that the Bluetooth system recognizes two types of link keys: semipermanent and temporary keys. There are two types of semipermanent link keys: unit keys and combination keys. Besides the combination key and the unit key, two other link key types are used: master and initialization keys.

A unit key is a link key that one device generates by itself and uses to pair with any other device, and a combination key is a key that a device generates in cooperation (combination) with another device. Therefore, the unit keys that a specific device shares with other paired devices are identical, whereas the combination keys are different for each pair of devices. Unit keys can only be safely used when there is full trust among the devices that are paired with a unit key, since every paired device can impersonate any other device holding the same unit key. For this reason, the use of unit keys has been deprecated in Bluetooth

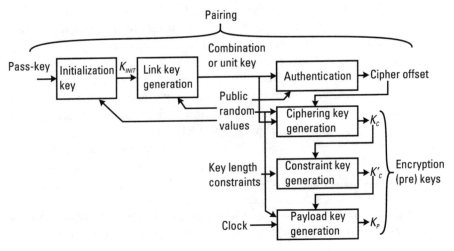

Figure 3.1 Overview of key management baseband events.

version 1.2. A further discussion on the vulnerabilities of the unit key can be found in Section 7.5.

A simple, yet important, step in the pairing procedure is the entering of the pass-key. From a baseband perspective, this means that the baseband cannot by itself complete the pairing but requires the input of the pass-key value. The pass-key is a byte string of 0 to 16 octets that is passed to the baseband. We come back to the details in Section 3.5, but for the moment one can imagine that the pass-key is entered via a man machine interface (MMI) interaction or a higher layer protocol.

3.4.1 Initialization key generation

Initialization keys are short lived, temporary keys that are used during the pairing of two devices. The initialization key, denoted by K_{INIT}, is the link key during the initialization process when no combination or unit key is present. K_{INIT} is computed by the algorithm E_{22} from the claimant's BD_ADDR, the entered pass-key $PKEY$ and its length L_{PKEY} (in octets), and a 128-bit random value IN_RAND. In fact, K_{INIT} is computed from the three values $PKEY'$, L'_{PKEY}, and IN_RAND, where[1]

$$PKEY' = \begin{cases} PKEY \cup BD\_ADDR & \text{when } L_{PKEY} \leq 10 \\ PKEY \cup BD\_ADDR[0...(15-L)] & \text{when } 10 < L_{PKEY} \leq 15 \quad (3.1) \\ PKEY & \text{when } L_{PKEY} = 16 \end{cases}$$

$$L'_{PKEY} = \min(L_{PKEY} + 6, 16) \qquad (3.2)$$

are derived from $PKEY$ and BD_ADDR by the padding mechanism described above when the length of $PKEY$ is less than 16 octets. Now we are able to compute K_{INIT} by

$$K_{INIT} = E_{22}(PKEY', IN\_RAND, L'_{PKEY}) \qquad (3.3)$$

The details of E_{22} are given in Section 4.2.3.

3.4.2 Unit key generation

Although the use of unit keys is deprecated due to the risks explained in Section 7.5, we describe for completeness, the baseband events that produce a unit key.

---

1. $x \cup y$ denotes the concatenation of the two strings x and y.

The starting point is the case of two devices that have no possession of a link key for their connection.

Suppose device A is the initiator and B is the responding device. If A does not yet hold a unit key, it starts by generating one. If the unit key of device A is used, the unit key is denoted by K_A. If, on the other hand, the unit key of unit B is used, the unit key is denoted by K_B.

The unit key K_A is computed by using the algorithm E_{21} from a locally generated (secret) 128-bit random value LK_RAND_A and the units' BD_ADDR; that is,

$$K_A = E_{21}\left(LK\_RAND_A, BD\_ADDR_A\right) \qquad (3.4)$$

The details of E_{21} are given in Section 4.2.2. Once the unit key is generated, it is sent to device B. However K_A is not sent by itself; instead, A sends

$$K'_A = K_A \oplus K_{INIT} \qquad (3.5)$$

Hence, the unit key is encrypted by using the initialization key. See Figure 3.2. Since device B also knows the initialization key, the recovery of the key is simply performed by the computation.

$$K'_A \oplus K_{INIT} = K_A \oplus K_{INIT} \oplus K_{INIT} = K_A$$

where the latter follows from the properties of the $\oplus$ (XOR) operation. Hence, unit B now also knows K_A.

If both device A and device B require the use of a unit key, there will be a conflict. Hence, if the semipermanent link key between A and B is a unit key, it must be the unit key of either unit A or unit B.

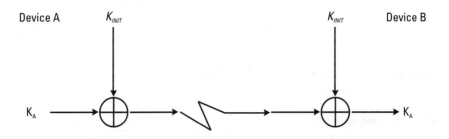

Figure 3.2 Process of transferring the unit key K_A to device B using the initialization key K_{INIT}. The key K_{INIT} is erased after the successful establishment of $K_{AB} = K_A$.

3.4.3 Combination key generation

The combination key is a link key that two pairing devices A and B generate together. Like the unit key, the combination key is generated when the two devices possess no common link key. The combination key is computed by combining their respective secret keys, K_A and K_B. The two keys are generated from locally generated (secret) 128-bit random values (LK_RAND_A and LK_RAND_B, respectively) and the units' BD_ADDR, using the algorithm E_{21}. To be more precise,

$$K_A = E_{21}\left(LK\_RAND_A, BD\_ADDR_A\right) \qquad (3.6)$$

$$K_B = E_{21}\left(LK\_RAND_B, BD\_ADDR_B\right) \qquad (3.7)$$

The combination key K_{AB} is then calculated as

$$K_{AB} = K_A \oplus K_B \qquad (3.8)$$

The latter calculation is only possible to perform if the units know the secret key of the other unit. This is realized by sending the secret random values LK_RAND_A and LK_RAND_B to each other, protected by the current link key K. The current link key might be a K_{INIT} or an existing combination key for the link. Thus, toward the final computation of K_{AB} the units send

$$C_A = LK\_RAND_A \oplus K, \quad \text{sent by } A \text{ to } B \qquad (3.9)$$

$$C_B = LK\_RAND_B \oplus K, \quad \text{sent by } B \text{ to } A \qquad (3.10)$$

Now, say unit A receives C_B and computes

$$C_B \oplus K = \left(LK\_RAND_B \oplus K\right) \oplus K = LK\_RAND_B$$

where the latter follows again from the properties of the $\oplus$ (XOR) operation. Hence, unit A now knows LK_RAND_B, and since it knows B's BD_ADDR value, it can compute K_B using (3.6). Unit B determines the combination key in a similar fashion from the received value C_A. Figure 3.3 illustrates the establishment of the combination key.

When two devices have exchanged a link key, the pairing is finalized with a (peer) authentication in which the devices prove to each other that they possess the correct link key. If the authentication fails, the pairing is not successful and a new pairing must be initiated.

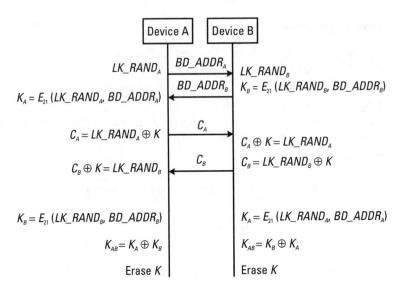

Figure 3.3 Process of generating the combination key K_{AB} between units A and B using the current link key K. The current link key K is erased after the successful establishment of K_{AB}.

3.4.4 Authentication

In the authentication process, a device will take either the role of claimant or verifier. In case of a mutual authentication, the roles will be interchanged in the process. Prior to the authentication, the host or user determines which device is the claimant and which device is the verifier. Which role to take depends on the security policy and security mode for each device. A more thorough discussion on security policies and security modes can be found in Section 2.5 and in Chapter 6.

Suppose device A is the verifier and device B is the claimant. Then A challenges device B by sending the random 128-bit value AU_RAND and expects from B the response

$$SRES = E_1\left(K, AU\_RAND, BD\_ADDR_B\right) \qquad (3.11)$$

where K is the exchanged link key and E_1 is the Bluetooth authentication function. E_1 is described in Section 4.2.1. The claimant B receives the challenge AU_RAND and sends A the response $SRES = E_1(K, AU\_RAND, BD\_ADDR_B)$. The verifier A receives $SRES'$ and compares its value with that of the expected $SRES$. If the values are equal, A declares that it has successfully authenticated device B. If the values differ, the authentication has failed. When A has successfully authenticated B, the LM may want to conduct a mutual authentication, in which case the above procedure is repeated with the roles of *A* and *B* interchanged. The random value used in the challenge of device *A* this time is a completely new random value.

It is important to note that it is not necessarily the master that starts as verifier. It is the application via the LM that determines the order in which authentication is performed and if one-way or mutual authentication is required. Figure 3.4 shows a mutual authentication.

Besides the peer authentication, the Bluetooth authentication procedure also results in the creation of the *authenticated ciphering offset* (ACO). The ACO is used when computing the ciphering key. In the case of mutual authentication, the ACO of the last authentication is retained. The ACO is produced by the mechanism E_1 at the same time *SRES* is computed. For details on the computation of *SRES* and ACO, see Section 4.2.1.

Finally, the Bluetooth authentication uses a simple method to reduce the impact of repeated erroneous authentications. This could, for example, be a component in a *denial-of-service* (DoS) attack. If authentication fails, a certain amount of time must elapse before the verifier will initiate a new attempt to the same claimant and before the claimant sends a response to an authentication attempt by a unit using the same identity as the unit that notified an authentication failure. For each additional authentication failure, the waiting interval should be exponentially increased until a certain maximum value is obtained. The Bluetooth specification speaks about a doubling of the waiting interval time. When no authentications take place, the waiting interval is exponentially reduced until a certain lowest value is reached. Moreover, if a successful authentication event takes place, the waiting interval may immediately be reset to the minimum value, To obtain some protection against a DoS attack, a Bluetooth

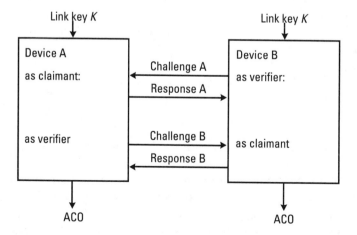

Figure 3.4 The mutual authentication process between devices *A* and *B* and the generation of the ACO.

device should keep a list containing, for each unit it has connected with, the corresponding waiting interval.

3.4.5   Master key generation

The master key is a temporary key that is used to protect data sent in broadcast messages where a master is communicating the same data to several slaves. See Chapter 5. The master key will replace the link key until the broadcast situation is terminated. The key K_{master} is computed by using the algorithm E_{22} and from two locally generated (secret) 128-bit random values LK_RAND1 and LK_RAND2:

$$K_{master} = E_{22}(LK\_RAND1, LK\_RAND2, 16) \qquad (3.12)$$

The value of K_{master} is sent to slave B. However, K_{master} is not sent by itself; instead, A sends first a third (but now public) 128-bit random value $RAND3$ followed by

$$K_{AB} = K_{master} \oplus K_{ovl} \qquad (3.13)$$

where K_{ovl} is an overlay key computed as

$$K_{ovl} = E_{22}(K, RAND3, 16) \qquad (3.14)$$

using the current link key K. Hence, the master key is encrypted by using the overlay key. See Figure 3.5. Since the slave B also knows the link key K and receives LK_RAND3, the recovery of the master key is simply performed by B through the computation

$$K_{AB} \oplus E_{22}(K, RAND3, 16) = K_{AB} \oplus K_{ovl}$$
$$= K_{master} \oplus K_{ovl} \oplus K_{ovl}$$
$$= K_{master}$$

The above procedure is carried out between the master and all the slaves involved in the broadcast. For each slave, a mutual authentication with the master will be performed using the master key as link key. The ACO values of these authentications should not replace the existing ACO values of the links between the master and slaves. These original ACO values are needed to recompute the original ciphering keys when the master terminates the broadcast and wants to

Master A   Slave B

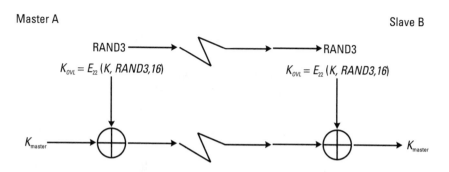

Figure 3.5 Process of transferring the master key K_{master} to slave device *B* using the overlay key K_{ovl}.

fall back to the previous link key. A replacement for the ACO is needed, which will be detailed in Section 3.6.1.

3.5 User interaction

The procedure for generating the link key is likely to include some manual user interaction in order to enter the pass-key. There are some issues involved that need to be considered when implementing this. One of the devices may lack a keyboard or keypad, so there is no practical means available for the user to enter the pass-key. In that case, this device must decide which pass-key to use. It can be a fixed pass-key (see Section 2.2), or, if it is possible for the device to announce the pass-key over another interface (e.g., a display), it can be a randomly chosen pass-key that changes for every pairing the Bluetooth device takes part in.

Another issue is the mapping of keyboard strokes to the actual pass-key, *PKEY*. Clearly, both ends must generate the same value. The internal key codes may differ between devices of different types (such as a computer and a mobile phone). Therefore, a standardized mapping is defined in the GAP [1]. The character representation of the pass-key at the user interface level is transformed according to the standard character encoding scheme UTF-8, and all decimal digits are within the Unicode range $0x00-0x7F$. Another requirement is that all devices capable of handling variable pass-keys (i.e., pass-keys entered at the user interface level) must support pass-keys consisting of decimal digits. Being capable of handling general characters is optional. In Table 3.1 we have listed an example of the mapping from a user-entered string to an actual pass-key.

Yet one problem becomes apparent when considering an example of pairing a Bluetooth-enabled keyboard with a desktop computer. Keyboards have different sets of characters for different alphabets. Moreover, the mapping of many common keys differs between languages (e.g., the U.S. QWERTY versus

Table 3.1

An Example of Two UTF-8 Encoded Pass-Keys

User-Entered String	Pass-Key (Hexadecimal)
'0123'	0x30313233
'Ärlig'	0xC384726C67

the French AZERTY keyboards). The keyboard itself usually lacks knowledge of what is printed on the key tops. Normally, a scan code is sent to the host, which interprets this code differently depending on the language setting. However, before the keyboard and the computer have been paired, the keyboard must do the interpretation by itself and it has to make some assumptions about the language in order to generate the correct *PKEY*. Then the best option for the computer is to only use numerical values in its random pass-key string, as the numerical keys tend to have the same scan codes for every language. The computer displays the chosen pass-key string on screen, and then the user enters this number on the keyboard in order to complete the pairing.

3.6   Cipher key generation

When encryption is desired, a ciphering key must be computed. In Bluetooth, the link key is not directly used as the key for the encryption mechanisms. Instead, the ciphering key is determined in several additional steps from the link key and is logically linked to the last authentication that has occurred between two devices through the ACO. In addition, the ciphering key is refreshed for each package that is transmitted. Since we want to explain the ciphering process in its entirety, we will in this section go stepwise through each detail of the ciphering key generation until the final key is fed into the E_0 stream cipher.

3.6.1   Encryption key K_c

Before encryption can commence, the encryption key must be computed. The encryption key K_C can be seen as a high-level encryption key from which the other ciphering keys are derived. The value of K_C is computed by using the algorithm E_3 from the current link key K, a 96-bit *ciphering offset* (COF), and a 128-bit random number *EN_RAND*. The value of COF equals the value of the authentication ciphering offset ACO, except when the current link key is a master key. In the latter case, COF is derived from the *BD_ADDR* of the master as

$$COF = \begin{cases} BD\_ADDR \| BD\_ADDR, & \text{when link is master key} \\ ACO & \text{otherwise} \end{cases} \quad (3.15)$$

Now K_C is given by

$$K_C = E_3(K, EN\_RAND, COF) \quad (3.16)$$

The ciphering activation always starts with a new computation of K_C and is a result of an explicit LM command. As a result, the encryption key is changed every time the encryption is activated. The algorithm E_3 is described in more detail in Section 4.2.4.

3.6.2 Constraint key K'_C

Bluetooth has a key strength constraining mechanism that reduces the 128-bit K_C to a 128-bit key whose effective key length may be less than 128 bits. Here, effective key length refers to the number of unknown (bit) combinations in the key. The constraining mechanism was introduced in Bluetooth as a result of export restrictions on encryption hardware. The resulting key is here called the constraint key and is denoted by K'_C. K'_C is determined for a given L by the computation

$$K'_C(x) = g_2^L(x)\{K_C(x) \ [\text{mod} \, g_1^L(x)]\} \quad (3.17)$$

where $K_C = (K_{C,0}, ..., K_{C,127})$, $K_{C,i} \in \{0,1\}$ and $K'_C = (K'_{C,0}, ..., K'_{C,127})$ and $K'_{C,i} \in \{0,1\}$,

$$K_C(x) = \sum_{i=0}^{127} K_{C,i} x^i$$

$$K'_C(x) = \sum_{i=0}^{127} K'_{C,i} x^i$$

and $(g_1^L(x), g_2^L(x))$ is a pair of polynomials over GF(2), that is, polynomials with coefficients that are elements of the finite field (Galois field) with 2 elements. Since the polynomials $K_C(x)$ and $K'_C(x)$ can also be viewed as polynomials over GF(2), the computation in (3.17) is performed using the arithmetic of polynomials over GF(2).[2] The modulo computation by $g_1(x)$ reduces $K_C(x)$ to a polynomial $h(x)$ of a degree less than the degree of $g_1(x)$. Thus the effective

---

2. Mathematicians would say that arithmetic is carried out in GF(2)[x] the ring of polynomials over GF(2).

number of unknown keys is reduced to at most $2^{\text{degree}[g_1(x)]}$. The multiplication of $h(x)$ by $g_2(x)$ results in a polynomial of a degree less than 128. Yet only $2^{\text{degree}[g_1(x)]}$ products can occur. Thus, depending on the degree of $g_1(x)$, this might be considerably less than 2^{128}, the number of all possible polynomials of degree less than 128. The polynomials $g_2(x)$ are chosen with an additional property that guarantees that if two different values of K_C result in two different $K_C'(x)$, the number of coefficients in which they differ is at least some given value. The latter value is denoted by D_{min}. There are 16 pairs of polynomials $[g_1^L(x), g_2^L(x)]$. Table 3.2 lists the pairs and the D_{min}^L of the resulting constrained key. The effective key length is $\leq 8L$.

Although the computations in (3.17) seem to be complicated, they are in fact very easily realized in a hardware circuit using a linear feedback/feedforward shift register with controllable taps. This fact, combined with the slight advantage of the guaranteed differences in the distinct K_C's, motivated the use of this way of constraining the encryption key.

The effective key length L (number of octets) is established via the encryption key size negotiation. As of Bluetooth version 1.2, there are two supported

Table 3.2
Table of Pairs of Key Constraining Polynomials and D_{min}^L Values (Or Upper Limits When Marked with an *)

L	Deg g_1^L		Deg g_2^L		D_{min}^L
1	8	00000000 00000000 00000000 0000011d	119	00e275a0 abd218d4 cf928b9b bf6cb08f	63
2	16	00000000 00000000 00000000 0001003f	112	0001e3f6 3d7659b3 7f18c258 cff6efef	48
3	24	00000000 00000000 00000000 010100db	104	000001be f66c6c3a b1030a5a 1919808b	44
4	32	00000000 00000000 00000001 000000af	96	00000001 6ab89969 de17467f d3736ad9	32
5	40	00000000 00000000 00000100 00000039	88	00000000 01630632 91da50ec 55715247	32*
6	48	00000000 00000000 00010000 00000291	77	00000000 00002c93 52aa6cc0 54468311	27*
7	56	00000000 00000000 01000000 00000095	71	00000000 000000b3 f7fffce2 79f3a073	24*
8	64	00000000 00000001 00000000 0000001b	63	00000000 00000000 a1ab815b c7ec8025	21*
9	72	00000000 00000100 00000000 00000609	49	00000000 00000000 0002c980 11d8b04d	15*
10	80	00000000 00010000 00000000 00000215	42	00000000 00000000 0000058e 24f9a4bb	14*
11	88	00000000 01000000 00000000 0000013b	35	00000000 00000000 0000000c a76024d7	11*
12	96	00000001 00000000 00000000 000000dd	28	00000000 00000000 00000000 1c9c26d9	9*
13	104	00000100 00000000 00000000 0000049d	21	00000000 00000000 00000000 0026d9e3	7*
14	112	00010000 00000000 00000000 0000014f	14	00000000 00000000 00000000 00004377	5*
15	120	01000000 00000000 00000000 000000e7	7	00000000 00000000 00000000 00000089	3
16	128	1 00000000 00000000 00000000 00000000	0	00000000 00000000 00000000 00000001	1

Note: Polynomials are given via their hexadecimal representation.

ways of doing this. The new and simple way is for the master to ask the slave what key lengths are supported using a bit vector (see Section 5.2). This is particularly useful in the case of broadcast encryption key negotiation. Alternatively, the master can proceed according to the procedure outlined below.

Each approved Bluetooth device must implement a maximal key size value L_{max}, $1 \leq L_{max} \leq 16$. In addition, each Bluetooth application should specify a lower value of L denoted as L_{min}. The effective key size L that the two devices A and B will use is determined through a negotiation that tries to find the largest key size that satisfies all the constraints on L between the master and slave devices. The negotiation starts with the master suggesting a length L_{sug} to a slave that equals the highest possible value for the master. If the constraints at the slave allow this suggested value of L, the suggested value is accepted as the value to be used. If the slave is not allowed to use the suggested value of L, the slave will send its L_{max} back to the master. Again, if the master allows this key length it will be used; otherwise, the master proposes the closest acceptable length that is smaller than this. The procedure is repeated with the master and slave alternating proposing the largest remaining key length. This hopefully leads finally to a key length that both master and slave can accept. However, it could be that the constraints are such that no key length exists that meets the size requirements of the slave and the master.

3.6.3　Payload key K_p

The payload key is the actual key that is used to (de)cipher the (incoming) outgoing packages. The value of K_p is computed per packet using the constraint key K'_C, and by a short run for E_0 loaded with K'_C, 26 bits of the current clock value, *BD_ADDR*, and a 128-bit random *EN_RAND*, Figure 3.6 shows that K_p is computed by the algorithm E_0 (see Section 4.4). In fact, K_p is formed by the state of the 4-bit register in the feedback path of E_0 and the last 128 bits of the key stream generated by E_0 when initialized with its input data and clocking the

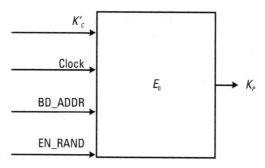

Figure 3.6　Process of generating the payload key K_p using the stream cipher algorithm E_0.

cipher to produce 240 symbols. Altogether, K_p is 132 bits in size. In Section 4.4.1 we return to the exact details.

3.7 Key databases

The Bluetooth combination key is used to protect the communication setup for one particular combination of two Bluetooth units. The key is unique for each combination of two Bluetooth units. Hence, there are as many combination keys as there are paired Bluetooth devices. Furthermore, all semipermanent keys (to which the combination key belongs) may be used for several repeated sessions between two units. Consequently, it should be possible to store semipermanent link keys in nonvolatile memory and it should be possible to retrieve the key upon request.

3.7.1 Unit keys generation requirements

The unit key is a 128-bit binary value that is generated as described in Section 3.4.2. It is of utmost importance that the random value used to generate the unit key is provided with a reliable random number generator with good statistical properties (see the recommendations in [2]). Furthermore, the random value used for the key generation should be discarded immediately after it has been used for the key generation. Once created, the unit key needs to be stored in a nonvolatile memory and should not be changed (see also Section 3.7.3).

3.7.2 Combination key generation requirements

The combination key, K_{AB}, is also a 128-bit binary value that needs to be stored in a nonvolatile memory (see Section 3.7.3). It may remain constant after it has been created. However, it is good security practice to periodically change the combination key.

The procedure for changing the key is exactly the same as in the initial generation of K_{AB} during the pairing procedure (see Section 3.4.3), where the current value of K_{AB} replaces K_{INIT} in the generation procedure. There is a specific HCI command that the host can use to enforce the key update: HCI Change Connection Link Key. Assume that the link manager of unit A receives a key change request through the HCI. This will cause the link manager to send an LMP comb key command to unit B. Unit B will respond with LMP comb key, and the key will be updated or it will reject the request by sending an LMP not accepted. After a successful generation of a new combination key, a mutual authentication must be performed in order to confirm that the same key has been created in both units. The host controllers of both units A

and *B* will then generate an `HCI Link Key Notification event` and the host controller of unit *A* will generate an `HCI Change Connection Link Key Complete event`. The `HCI Link Key Notification event` of unit *A* contains the device address of unit *B* (and vice versa) and the new value of the link key. The host can choose to store the new key in its own database, or it can be stored by the link controller (see Section 3.7.3 below). The `HCI Change Connection Link Key Complete event` is only used to indicate whether the change of the link key succeeded or not. A message sequence example of combination key change is shown in Figure 3.7.

The combination key update policy of a unit should be part of the unit security policy. This security policy might be different for different units. If K_{AB} is used very often, it needs to be updated regularly. Similarly, if there exists an indication that K_{AB} has been compromised, it should of course be changed.

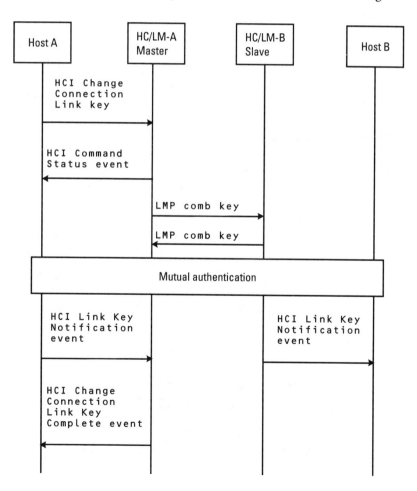

Figure 3.7 Message sequence chart for a change of the combination key.

3.7.3   Key databases

Format and usage

To retrieve the correct link key upon request from the host or unit, the semipermanent link keys must be stored in a database. Consider one Bluetooth unit, say *A*. Below we discuss the database format and usage from the perspective of this unit.

The link key is identified by the device address of the other unit in the link. In this case, *A* needs to store as many keys as the number of performed pairings with distinguishing units. Consequently, the simplest form of database is a list of key entries where each entry only has two values, the device address, and the corresponding link key. This is shown in the database example in Table 3.3, where the device addresses and key values are written in hexadecimal notation. The device address is a 48-bit long (12 hexadecimal digits) value, while the key is 128 bits long (32 hexadecimal digits).

If *A* is always using a unit key, there is no need for a link key database, since the same key is used for all connections (independent of the device address of the other units). We might have a situation where the unit would like to issue unit keys for some connections while still using combination keys for other connections. However, in practice, there would in most cases then be enough storage capacity for always using a combination key and not using unit keys at all (see also the general discussion regarding unit keys in Section 7.5).

If we use the simple database format of Table 3.3, no information is given of the type of semipermanent key that is used (i.e., unit or combination key). However, a key in the table entry might be a unit key. Since a unit key is not as secure as a combination key, we might want to enforce a more restricted security policy (see Chapter 6 for more information on the usage of security policies in Bluetooth). Hence, it might be good to add one extra information field containing the key type to each entry in the table. We show this in the database example in Table 3.4. In this example, all listed keys except the last one are combination keys.

In addition to this basic information, it is advisable to add some redundancy to the database entries so that errors can be detected. The reasons for this

Table 3.3
An Example of a Link Key Database

Device Address	Key
10FA48C7DE52	1B4D5698AE374FDE8390912463DFE3AB
047F6BB427EA	FE729425BC9A95D39132BDE275917823
A5EE29667190	091827AD41D4E48D29CBE82615D18490
⋮	⋮
068935F6B3E2	126304467592CD71FF19B4428133AD8E

Table 3.4

Link Key Database Example with Key Type Information

Device Address	Key	Key Type
10FA48C7DE52	1B4D5698AE374FDE8390912463DFE3AB	C
047F6BB427EA	FE729425BC9A95D39132BDE275917823	C
A5EE29667190	091827AD41D4E48D29CBE82615D18490	C
⋮	⋮	⋮
068935F6B3E2	126304467592CD71FF19B4428133AD8E	U

U = unit key; C = combination key.

will be discussed in the next section. For instance, a simple 8-bit CRC code can be added to each row of Table 3.4.

Corrupted database

The link key database might for some reason become corrupted. The probability of having corrupted databases depends on the type of storage medium and the storage protection mechanisms. If a device address field is damaged, it might result in key lookup error. If the corrupted key entry is detected when the unit is about to send an authentication (acting as verifier), the error can be handled internally by the unit. In this case, it should be possible for the user (if desired) to demand a new pairing and derive a new link key, and the unit will initiate a new pairing by sending the LMP command `LMP in rand`.

If the corrupted key entry is detected after an authentication request by the other unit, the unit should return `LMP not accepted` after it has received the `LMP au rand` (see Section 3.3) with the reason "key missing," as illustrated in Figure 3.8.

The behavior in this case is up to the unit requesting the authentication. It might demand a new pairing by sending an `LMP in rand`, or it might refuse the connection and detach the link. However, in order to handle corrupted databases, there should always be the possibility for the user to make a new pairing of the two devices. Hence, it must be possible for the user to find out the reason for a failed link setup.

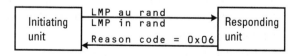

Figure 3.8 Authentication after key lookup failure by claimant unit. The claimant unit returns "LMP not accepted" with reason code 0×6 (i.e., "key missing").

Storage

There are several different options for where and how to store the link key database. The Bluetooth controller might have the capability to cache a limited set of recently used link keys. However, the most common situation is that the link key database is handled by the host and that the necessary link keys are passed to the Bluetooth controller (i.e., the Bluetooth module), for example, through the defined HCI command HCI Write Stored Link Key. This command can be used to transfer one or several link keys from the host to the Bluetooth controller. The number of possible keys is determined by the link key storage capacity of the Bluetooth controller.

It is also possible that the Bluetooth controller itself completely handles the link key database. However, this is not an especially secure solution, since there is no secure HCI mechanism (involving user authentication) defined for "opening" the key database. This problem will be discussed in Section 7.4.1.

Hence, we will below assume that the key database is handled by the host. If the host handles the security database, but the keys are passed to a link key database in the controller, it is good security practice to delete the keys from the controller database after they have been used. This can be done through the HCI command HCI Delete Stored Link Key.

The Bluetooth specification does not contain any recommendations for how a host should handle the key database. Here we discuss some issues and possible solutions. In Section 7.4 we will come back to the risks that one may face if storage is not handled correctly.

There are two important security issues regarding key storage: access control and secure storage. In order to prevent a hostile user or software in control of the host to read and/or modify the link keys, the access to the keys should be restricted. Furthermore, depending on the security requirements, it should not be easy for a hostile user to physically read out the keys from the storage medium. It must still be possible for authorized users to open the database. Hence, there must be mechanisms in place for some type of user authentication. Simple forms of user authentication are PIN- or password-based authentication mechanisms. We discuss three different approaches to database storage that provide user authentication through a PIN or password.

A highly secure storage medium is an *integrated circuit card* (ICC). In order to access information on an ICC, the user is often required to enter a PIN. Hence, an ICC provides both a user authentication mechanism and secure storage. Whenever, this security level is demanded and affordable, this would be the preferred solution for storing the link key database.

If an ICC is not available, an alternative is to store the database encrypted on a general storage medium available to the host (like a hard disk or flash memory). If the database should be encrypted, there must be an encryption key available. Obviously, if this key is stored in clear text, there is no need for encrypting the database, since it will be easy for anybody familiar with the system to decrypt the keys. A possible solution to this is to derive the key from a *password-based key derivation function*. A key derivation function produces a key from a password and other parameters. This requires a user password input. Hence, indirectly, one will get a form of user authentication. Only the legitimate user will (hopefully) be able to derive the database encryption key. A widely used scheme for password-based encryption is the RSA PKCS#5 "Password-Based Cryptography Standard" [3]. The standard suggests encryption based on the DES or RC2 block cipher algorithms[3], but other block ciphers like SAFER+ or the Advanced Encryption Standard (AES) are useful too.

Finally, a third (even less secure) storage alternative for the host is to have no explicit protection of the key database at all. If there is a login procedure required to activate the host, one might consider that this also gives enough protection for the Bluetooth link key database.

3.7.4 Semipermanent keys for temporary use

In some situations, one Bluetooth unit is temporarily connected to another unit. Examples of such situations are public access points, public printers, or the exchange of documents between two business people. Even if these connections will only be used once, there is a need to protect the communication. Hence, the units must derive the necessary link and encryption keys. The Bluetooth standard does not make any distinction between temporary connections and other connections. Thus, it is up to the host implementation to take care of temporary link keys in a proper way. There is no need to store these keys, since it is highly probable that they are not going to be used anymore. Furthermore, depending on the host (link key) security policy, there might be a security risk if the temporary link keys used will automatically provide the unit access at a later occasion. It is good security practice for the user to be able to decide whether a link key should be stored in the link key database or not (and in some circumstances also for how long a time). Clearly, each implementation must provide some means for the user to remove stored link keys.

References

[1] Bluetooth Special Interest Group, *Specification of the Bluetooth System, Version 1.1, Profiles, Part K:1 Generic Access Profile*, February 2001.

---

3. DES and RC2 are two block ciphers; see [2] for more details.

[2]   van Oorschot, P. C., A. J. Menezes, and S. A. Vanstone, *Handbook of Applied Cryptography*, Boca Raton, FL: CRC Press, 1997.

[3]   RSA Data Security Inc., Redwood City, CA, *PKCS #5: Password-Based Cryptography Standard, Version 2.0*, March 1999.

4

Algorithms

In this chapter, the internal workings of the Bluetooth cryptographic algorithms will be described. These algorithms can be divided into two groups. On one hand we have the four algorithms E_1, E_{21}, E_{22}, and E_3, which all use the same underlying 128-bit block cipher SAFER+. On the other hand, we have the Bluetooth encryption mechanism E_0, which uses a stream cipher with a 132-bit initial state. Because of SAFER+'s and E_0's central position, we will focus in this chapter on describing these two algorithms. Some implementation aspects will be discussed at the end of the chapter. We start by returning to the basic description of cryptographic algorithms from Chapter 1.

4.1 Crypto algorithm selection

4.1.1 Block ciphers

In Chapter 1, block ciphers and stream ciphers were introduced as reversible transformations to encrypt plaintext information into cipher text. In Chapter 3, we saw that the key management in the Bluetooth systems involves several key derivation and generation methods. By simply looking at the way the key derivation algorithms E_1, E_{21}, E_{22}, and E_3 are defined (as mappings from inputs to an output), one can see that these are very similar to block ciphers. It is rather easy to modify a block cipher for use in these four algorithms. This is typical and block ciphers are therefore often found in key derivation mechanisms for other systems. Since keys in the Bluetooth system are 128 bits long, it is natural to use a block cipher that can transform 128-bit data with a 128-bit key, since keys can then be directly used as data input as well. Besides this interface requirement, one wants a block cipher with a high strength level and that is cryptographically well understood. There are a number of block ciphers available that would fit into these requirements. An additional requirement is that the use of the algorithm was free, that is, not limited by patent rights or license fees. The designers of the Bluetooth system chose SAFER+. The algorithm was at the time of selection for Bluetooth one of the contenders[1] for the AES. It was taken out of the competition mainly because of the results in performance measurements using reference implementations and because the 256-bit key version had a weakness that reduced the effective key size somewhat. Yet SAFER+ was available with very thorough cryptanalysis using state-of-the-art block cipher analysis techniques. The latter, in combination with the experience of its predecessor SAFER [1], convinced the Bluetooth designers to put their trust in SAFER+. As of today, no weaknesses in SAFER+ have been reported that constitute a threat to its use in Bluetooth.

4.1.2 Stream ciphers

Stream ciphers are ideal in communication systems, since they very easily handle plaintexts of various length. Block ciphers can be used as well but require padding schemes. Furthermore, traditionally, stream ciphers have been designed with (low) implementation complexity in mind. There are mainly two approaches toward designing a stream cipher: direct or indirect via a block cipher. This split is not very well defined, and it may well happen that one cannot tell which design type a specific construction belongs to.

In a block cipher–based design, the block cipher is complemented with memory registers to keep a state and with a feedback mechanism to create an altogether autonomous finite state machine. The overall key to the stream cipher system is often used as the key to the block cipher but could also determine the initial state of the registers. To be attractive, this kind of design requires the block cipher to be very implementation friendly in either software or hardware or both. An example of such a design is the Universal Mobile Telecommunications System (UMTS) encryption algorithm f8 [2], which uses the KASUMI block cipher. In a direct design, one constructs the autonomous finite state machine directly, potentially offering an easier way for keeping implementation complexity down. Compared to block ciphers, it is somewhat more difficult to meaningfully define the strength requirements of a stream cipher. For our purposes it is sufficient to state that even if the attackers have access to a very long key stream, they should not be able to recover the key that was used to generate that key stream. Let us now turn to the Bluetooth system.

---

1. It was submitted by Cylink, Corp., Sunnyvale, CA, and designed by J. L. Massey and G. H. Khachatrian.

The stream cipher E_0 is based on a direct design and uses a Bluetooth proprietary algorithm that has its roots in the so-called summation combiner stream cipher. This was a stream cipher that was proposed by Massey and Rueppel [3, 4] in the mid-1980s. Its strengths and weaknesses are well understood through the works of [5–7]. From that time to the time of writing, the most powerful attacks on this type of stream ciphers are the correlation attacks in combination with exhaustive search over a limited key space (this is sometimes also referred to as *initial guessing*). The original summation combiner design was modified to reduce the correlations that are used in the attacks by adding additional logic. In Section 4.1.2, we will describe this and its consequences in more detail. The works of Golic [7] and Hermelin and Nyberg [8] lead to the conclusion that a summation combiner type of stream cipher with a total state space of K bits (2^K states) will provide only about $K/2$ bits in security when sufficient key stream data is available. As we will see later, more recent cryptanalysis shows that the E_0 cipher is weaker than this. Therefore, the frequent rekeying in Bluetooth and the rather short generated key streams are essential for keeping the threat of (correlation) attacks at a safe distance.

4.2 SAFER+

The SAFER+ block cipher has its roots in the SAFER block cipher. The original SAFER cipher has been analyzed (see [9]), and apart from a correction in the original key scheduling, SAFER is still a safe algorithm, provided a sufficient number of rounds is used. SAFER is, however, a cipher working on 64-bit data blocks, which is too small for use in Bluetooth. SAFER+ uses a round construction similar to that of SAFER, consisting of pseudo-Hadamard transforms, substitution tables, and subkey insertion (see [1]). An important improvement in SAFER+ is the introduction of the so-called "Armenian Shuffle" permutation, which boosts the diffusion of single-bit modifications in the input data. In fact, the diffusion in SAFER+ is already very good after one round. This is a highly desirable property of any good block cipher. In [10], this property is proved along with other state-of-the-art cryptanalysis. For a recent summary of cryptanalytic results, see [11].

SAFER+ has two subsystems: the encryption subsystem and the key scheduling subsystem. It shares this setup with many other block cipher algorithms. Let us first have a look at key scheduling. See Figure 4.1. The task of key scheduling is to provide key material, called a *round key*, for each of the encryption rounds in the encryption subsystem. Each round key consists of two vectors of 16 octets. The key scheduling borrows ideas from the strengthened schedule of SAFER. See [9]. The last round key, K_{17}, is a single vector of 16 octets that are

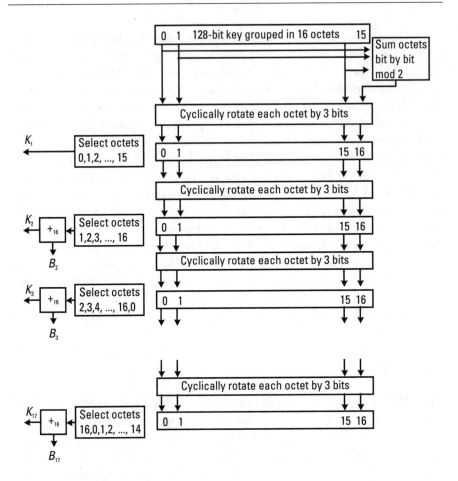

Figure 4.1 SAFER key scheduling.

"added" to the output of the last round. See Figure 4.2. Each of the 16-octet[2] vectors $K_i = (K_i[0], K_i[1], \ldots, K_i[15])$, except K_1, are offset by a bias $B_i = (b_i[0], b_i[1], \ldots, b_i[15])$, $i = 2, 3, \ldots, 17$ using modulo 256 addition. The bias vectors are defined by

$$b_i[j] = \left[\left(45^{\left(45^{17i+j+1} \bmod 257 \right)} \bmod 257 \right) \bmod 256 \right], \quad \text{for } j = 0, 1, \ldots, 15 \quad (4.1)$$

---

2. We will here and in the following regard octets as being integer numbers 0, 1, . . ., 255 or as being eight-dimensional binary valued vectors, whichever is suitable in the context of usage. The binary vector representation corresponds to the radix-2 representation of the integer value of the octet; that is, the octet 131 is also written as 10000011.

The round keys are fed into SAFER+'s round mechanism where they are added into the round data. The addition is done by intertwined modulo 256 and XOR additions. See Figure 4.2. The SAFER+ uses two tables, referred to as E and L, that implement the mappings:

$$E, L: \quad \{0, 1, \ldots, 255\} \rightarrow \{0, 1, \ldots, 255\} \tag{4.2}$$

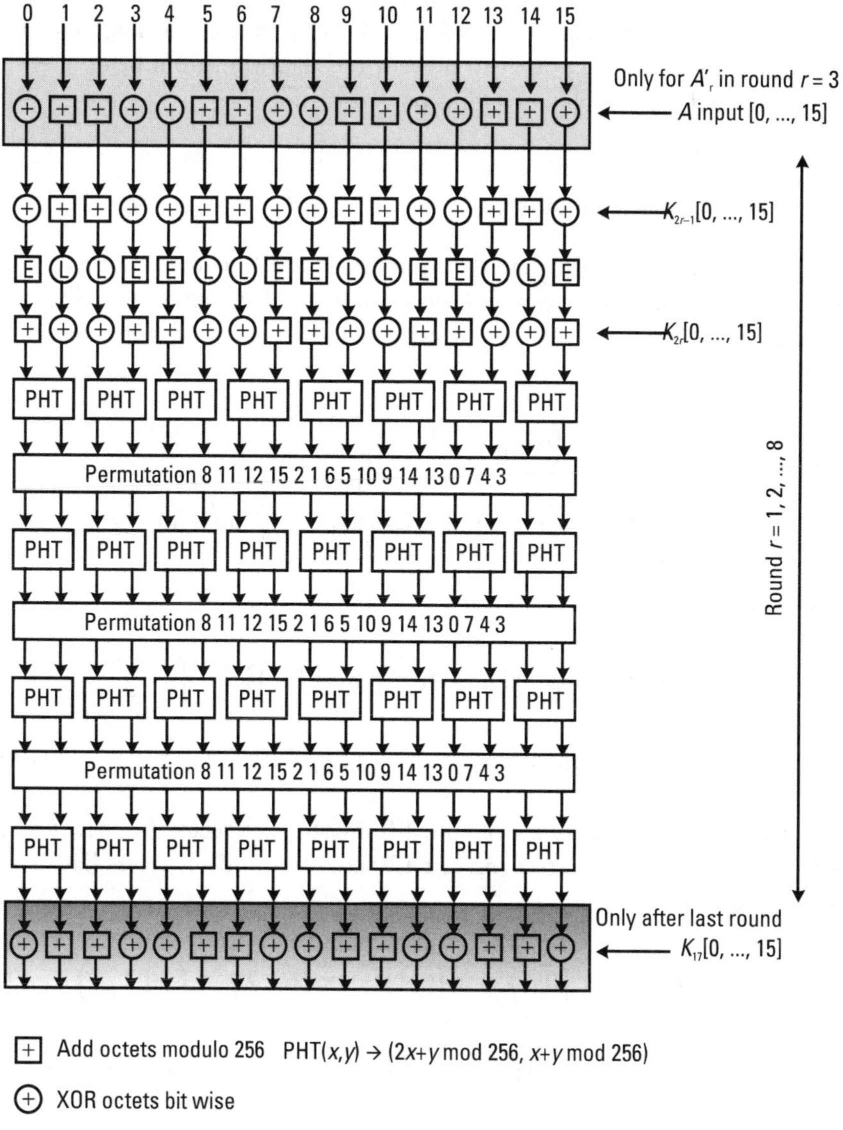

Figure 4.2 One round of SAFER+ with Bluetooth adoptions. The permutation maps output 0 to input 8, output 1 to input 11, and so on.

$$E: \quad x \mapsto \left(45^x \bmod 257\right) \bmod 256 \qquad (4.3)$$

$$L: \quad x \mapsto y \text{ such that } x = E(y) \qquad (4.4)$$

These two mappings introduce nonlinearity. Figure 4.2 also shows the modification of SAFER+ used in the Bluetooth A'_r algorithm. A'_r is SAFER+ with the modification that the original input to the algorithm is also added to the input of the third round. This makes A'_r into a noninvertible mapping. This modification was made in order to prevent the algorithm from being used for encryption and avoid problems with export regulations.

4.2.1 Authentication algorithm E_1

We recall from Chapter 3 that algorithm E_1 is the Bluetooth authentication algorithm. It is called a *message authentication code* (MAC) algorithm. The algorithm E_1 is built around SAFER+, which for convenience is denoted by A_r and defined as

$$A_r: \quad \{0, 1\}^{128} \times \{0, 1\}^{128} \rightarrow \{0, 1\}^{128} \qquad (4.5)$$

$$(k, x) \mapsto y = \text{SAFER+}\left(\text{key} = k, \text{input} = x\right) \qquad (4.6)$$

Now we define E_1 in a few steps. First let

$$E_1 : \{0, 1\}^{128} \times \{0, 1\}^{128} \times \{0, 1\}^{48} \rightarrow \{0, 1\}^{32} \times \{0, 1\}^{96} \qquad (4.7)$$

$$(K, RAND, \text{address}) \mapsto (SRES, \text{ACO}) \qquad (4.8)$$

Here *SRES* and ACO are obtained from 16-octet vector *hash* (K, *RAND*, address, 6) as the first 4 octets and last 12 octets, respectively. Here hash is the function defined by

$$hash: \quad \{0, 1\}^{128} \times \{0, 1\}^{128} \times \{0, 1\}^{8 \times L} \times \{6, 12\} \rightarrow \left(\{0, 1\}^8\right)^{16} \qquad (4.9)$$

$$(K, I1, I2, L) \mapsto A'_r\left(\tilde{K}, E(I2, L) +_{16} \left[A_r(K, I1) \oplus_{16} I1\right]\right) \qquad (4.10)$$

where $E(I2, L)$ is an expansion of the L octet vector $I2$ into a 16-octet (128 bits) vector, defined by

$$E: \ \{0,1\}^{8 \times L} \times \{6,12\} \to \left(\{0,1\}^8\right)^{16} \tag{4.11}$$

$$\left(X[0,\ldots,L-1],L\right) \mapsto \left(X[i \bmod L; i=0,\ldots,15]\right) \tag{4.12}$$

The function *hash* is also used by the algorithm E_3, where $L = 12$ is used. For E_1, L is always 6 octets. The SAFER+ algorithm is used twice: once as defined, that is, A_r, and a second time slightly modified by adding the input octets into the input of the third round. The latter is referred to as algorithm A'_r. The observant reader has of course noticed that the key K to A'_r is not the same as the key K that is used for A_r. The key $\tilde{K}$ is derived from an offset of K. The offset is defined as follows:

$$
\begin{aligned}
\tilde{K}[0] &= \left(K[0] + 233\right) \bmod 256, & \tilde{K}[1] &= \left(K[1] \oplus 229\right) \\
\tilde{K}[2] &= \left(K[2] + 233\right) \bmod 256, & \tilde{K}[3] &= \left(K[3] \oplus 193\right) \\
\tilde{K}[4] &= \left(K[4] + 179\right) \bmod 256, & \tilde{K}[5] &= \left(K[5] \oplus 167\right) \\
\tilde{K}[6] &= \left(K[6] + 149\right) \bmod 256, & \tilde{K}[7] &= \left(K[7] \oplus 131\right) \\
\tilde{K}[0] &= \left(K[0] \oplus 233\right), & \tilde{K}[1] &= \left(K[1] + 229\right) \bmod 256 \\
\tilde{K}[2] &= \left(K[2] \oplus 223\right), & \tilde{K}[3] &= \left(K[3] + 193\right) \bmod 256 \\
\tilde{K}[4] &= \left(K[4] \oplus 179\right), & \tilde{K}[5] &= \left(K[5] + 167\right) \bmod 256 \\
\tilde{K}[6] &= \left(K[6] \oplus 149\right), & \tilde{K}[7] &= \left(K[7] + 131\right) \bmod 256
\end{aligned}
\tag{4.13}
$$

Figure 4.3 summarizes the steps that form the algorithm E_1. The figure also shows how the output of the hash function is split into two parts. The first 4 octets form the response *SRES* and the remaining 12 octets form the authentication offset ACO.

4.2.2 Unit key algorithm E_{21}

The algorithm E_{21} used for the unit key derivation is built around A'_r. See Figure 4.4(a). Formally it is specified as

$$E_{21}: \{0,1\}^{128} \times \{0,1\}^{48} \to \{0,1\}^{128} \tag{4.14}$$

$$\left(RAND, \text{address}\right) \mapsto A'_r \left(RAND[0..14] \cup \left(RAND[15] \oplus 6\right), Q\right) \tag{4.15}$$

where $Q = \cup_{i=0}^{15} \text{address}[i \bmod 6]$

Because A'_r is used instead of the original SAFER+, algorithm E_{21} cannot be used directly as an invertible encryption algorithm.

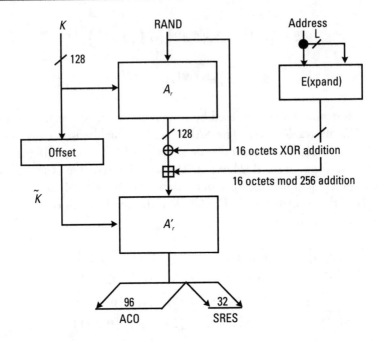

Figure 4.3 The structure of E_1.

4.2.3 Initial key algorithm E_{22}

The algorithm E_{22} used for the initial key derivation is also built around A_r' but differs slightly from E_{22}. See Figure 4.4(b). Let N denote the pass-key length. Formally, E_{22} is specified as

$$E_{22}: \quad \left(\{0,1\}^8\right)^{N'} \times \{0,1\}^{128} \times \{1,2,\ldots,16\} \to \{0,1\}^{128} \quad (4.16)$$

$$\left(PKEY', RAND, N'\right) \mapsto A_r'\left(X,Y\right) \quad (4.17)$$

$$X = \cup_{i=0}^{15} PKEY'\left[i \bmod N'\right] \quad (4.18)$$

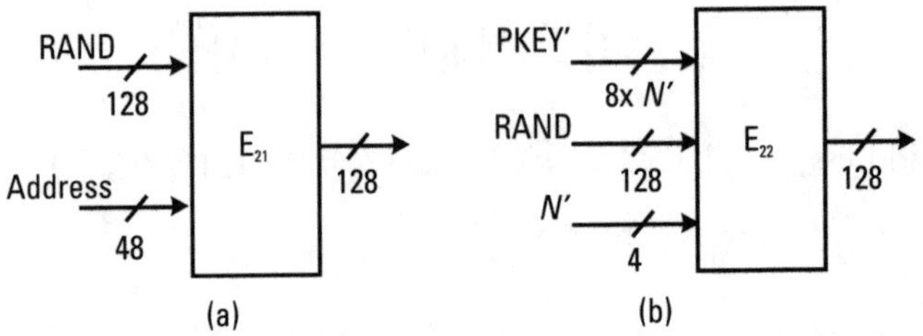

Figure 4.4 Block diagrams of (a) E_{21}, and (b) E_{22}.

$$Y = RAND[0...14] \cup (RAND[15] \oplus N') \qquad (4.19)$$

where $N' = \min(16, 6 + N)$ is the length of $PKEY'$ in octets and where

$$PKEY' = \begin{cases} PKEY[0,...,N-1] \\ \qquad \cup BD\_ADDR[0,...,\min(5,15-N)] & N < 16 \\ PKEY[0,...,N-1] & N = 16 \end{cases} \qquad (4.20)$$

4.2.4 Encryption key algorithm E_3

Finally, the encryption key generation algorithm E_3 is defined as

$$E3 : \{0,1\}^{128} \times \{0,1\}^{128} \times \{0,1\}^{96} \rightarrow \{0,1\}^{128} \qquad (4.21)$$

$$(K, RAND, COF) \mapsto hash(K, RAND, COF, 12) \qquad (4.22)$$

where hash is the function defined in (4.9). The reader should remember, though, that this encryption key K_C is not used directly. K_C is used to derive the constraint key that is input into the ciphering algorithm E_0, which we describe in the next section. One may notice that E_{21} and E_{22} are very similar. This is a design choice to simplify the implementation. Figure 4.5 gives the block diagram of E_3.

4.3 Encryption engine

We already informally discussed the encryption engine E_0 in Bluetooth at the beginning of this chapter. Abstractly E_0 is a so-called autonomous finite state machine. Loaded with an initial state, it will on every clock cycle move to a new state and produce one single output bit of the key stream. The ciphering key that is loaded into the encryption engine is the constraint key K_C'. Apart from

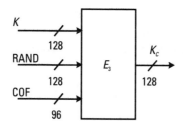

Figure 4.5 Block diagram of E_3.

the constraint key, the initial state is determined by 26 bits of the current clock value, *BD_ADDR*, and a 128-bit random *EN_RAND*. As explained in Section 3.6.3, one first determines a payload key by running E_0 for 200 clock cycles. One can regard this as a means of mixing the initial state data. Of the 200 generated output symbols (bits), the last 128 bits are retained and subsequently loaded back into E_0 as its initial state for the process of generating the key stream symbols that are used for encryption (alternatively, for decryption) of the outgoing (incoming) data.

For the sake of exposition, we first describe the construction of E_0 and will return to a description of the initialization steps after we have more knowledge of the construction.

4.4   Ciphering algorithm E_0

The core of E_0 is built around four independent linear feedback registers and a finite state machine as a combining circuitry. The latter is needed to introduce sufficient nonlinearity to make it difficult to recompute the initial state from observing key stream data. In Chapter 7 we will come back to the trade-offs that are involved here when we discuss the strengths and weaknesses in the Bluetooth security system. The four linear feedback registers LFSR$_i$, i = 1, 2, 3, 4 are each fully characterized by the following four feedback polynomials [12]:

$$\text{LFSR}_1: \quad f_1(t) = t^{25} + t^{20} + t^{12} + t^8 + 1 \qquad (4.23)$$

$$\text{LFSR}_2: \quad f_2(t) = t^{31} + t^{24} + t^{16} + t^{12} + 1 \qquad (4.24)$$

$$\text{LFSR}_3: \quad f_3(t) = t^{33} + t^{28} + t^{24} + t^4 + 1 \qquad (4.25)$$

$$\text{LFSR}_4: \quad f_4(t) = t^{39} + t^{36} + t^{28} + t^4 + 1 \qquad (4.26)$$

Note that the sum of the degrees of these four polynomials is 128. The output sequence $X_1 = (x_{10}, x_{11}, \ldots)$ of register 1, say, when assuming that we clock the register infinitely long, can be expressed by the formal power series:

$$X_1(t) = \sum_{i=0}^{\infty} x_{1i} t^i$$

From the theory of linear feedback registers we know that we can write

$$X_1(t) = \frac{g_1(t)}{f_1(t)}$$

for some polynomial $g_1(t)$ (with binary coefficients) of degree less than the degree of $f_1(t)$. See, for example, [12]. The polynomial division is carried out by using ordinary polynomial arithmetic but using modulo 2 arithmetic in the coefficients. It is the linear feedback circuit that implements this division operation using delay elements to hold the coefficients and XOR gates to do the modulo 2 operations. Each of the four polynomials is a so-called maximum length polynomial, which means that the periods of the output sequences of LFSRs have periods $2^{\text{degree}f_i} - 1$, $i = 1, 2, 3, 4$ [12]. That is, we have

$$\text{period } X_1 : P_1 = 2^{25} - 1 \tag{4.27}$$

$$\text{period } X_2 : P_2 = 2^{31} - 1 \tag{4.28}$$

$$\text{period } X_3 : P_3 = 2^{33} - 1 \tag{4.29}$$

$$\text{period } X_4 : P_4 = 2^{39} - 1 \tag{4.30}$$

As we will see later, the polynomials are in fact maximum length *windmill polynomials* (see Section 4.5). The windmill property can be exploited in a hardware or software realization of the LFSR.

The four sequences $X_1, \ldots, X_4$ are fed symbol by symbol into a so-called summation combiner which adds the four input symbols together as if they were natural numbers, adds the result to a number c_t, depending on the summation combiner's state, and obtains a sum s_t, $t = 0, 1, \ldots$. Formally we have

$$s_t = x_{1t} + x_{2t} + x_{3t} + x_{4t} + c_t \in \{0, 1, \ldots, 7\}$$

because c_t takes on only the values 0, 1, 2, 3. The output symbol z_t is the binary result obtained by setting

$$z_t = s_t \bmod 2 = x_{1t} \oplus x_{2t} \oplus x_{3t} \oplus x_{4t} \oplus (c_t \bmod 2)$$

The new value c_{t+1} is obtained by rewriting[3] first the result of the computation

---

3. The Bluetooth core specification defines the computation of the new state in a different manner using the finite field representation of the values of *ct*. The manner defined here is equivalent to the one in the core specification but avoids the use of finite fields.

$$u_{t+1} = \left\lfloor \frac{s_t}{2} \right\rfloor$$

as a binary vector $\mathbf{u}_{t+1}$ (of dimension 2) and then setting

$$\mathbf{c}_{t+1} = \begin{pmatrix} c_{0t+1} \\ c_{1t+1} \end{pmatrix} = \mathbf{u}_{t+1} \oplus \begin{pmatrix} 1 & 0 \\ 0 & 1 \end{pmatrix} \mathbf{c}_t \oplus \begin{pmatrix} 1 & 1 \\ 1 & 0 \end{pmatrix} \mathbf{c}_{t-1} \qquad (4.31)$$

(computing modulo 2 in the coefficients), and, finally, defining the mapping:

$$\downarrow : c_t = 2c_{1t} + c_{ot} \qquad (4.32)$$

A close inspection shows that (4.31) defines a linear infinite impulse response (IIR) filter that scrambles the state variables. We will later see that the IIR filter lowers the correlation factor that is an important parameter in the so-called correlation attack. In Figure 4.6 the core of E_0 is shown schematically.

Missing in Figure 4.6 are the initialization parts which will be described in the next sections. Before we discuss the initialization, we want to point out that the sequence $V = (v_0, v_1, \ldots)$ with

$$v_t = x_{1t} \oplus x_{2t} \oplus x_{3t} \oplus x_{4t}$$

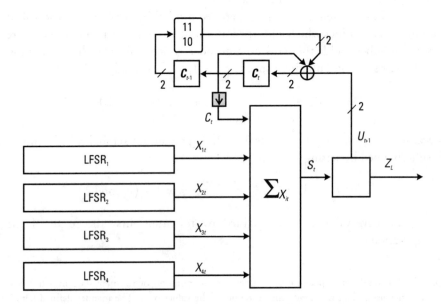

Figure 4.6 The schematics of the E_0 core engine.

has period $P = (P_1 P_2 P_3 P_4)/7$ and not $P_1 P_2 P_3 P_4$ due to the fact that the periods P_3 and P_4 have 7 as their greatest common divisor. Hence, if we assume that none of the LFSRs is initialized with an all zero state, there are 7 cycles of length $P \approx 2^{125.2}$ [13].

4.4.1 Initialization

The initialization of E_0 prior to the payload key computation is rather involved. The key stream generator needs to be loaded with the initial values for the four LFSRs (altogether 128 bits) and the 4 bits that specify the values of c_0 and c_{-1}. This 132-bit initial value is derived from four inputs: the constraint key K'_C, a *BD_ADDR* value, and a clock CLK value by using the key stream generator itself. The length of K'_C is 128 bits. With the generator, 200 stream cipher bits are generated, of which the last 128 bits are fed back into the key stream generator as the initial values of the four LFSRs. The values of c_0 and c_{-1} are kept. The details of the initialization are as follows:

1. Shift in the three inputs K'_C, the *BD_ADDR* address, the clock CLK bits, and the 6-bit (decimal) constant 113 (208 bits total).

   a. Open all switches shown in Figure 4.7.

   b. Arrange input bits as shown in Figure 4.7. ADR[i] denotes the bytes of *BD_ADDR*, and similarly CLK[i] denotes the relevant bytes of the clock.

   c. Set the initial states of the LFSRs to zero ($t = 0$).

   d. Start to shift in the input bits.

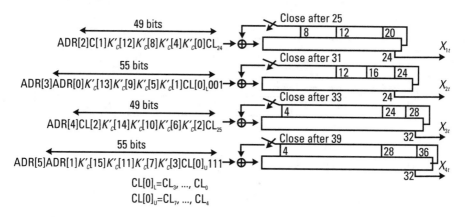

Figure 4.7 First loading of the four LFSRs.

e. Close feedback switch of LFSR$_1$ after 25 clock instants, that of LFSR$_2$ after 31 clock instants, that of LFSR$_3$ after 33 clock instants, and that of LFSR$_4$ after 39 clock instants.

f. At $t = 39$, set bits $c_{39} = 0$ and $c_{38} = 0$.

g. Continue to shift in remaining inputs bits. Note: When finished, LFSR$_1$ has effectively clocked 30 times with feedback closed. LFSR$_2$ 24 times, LFSR$_3$ 22 times, and LFSR$_4$ 16 times.

2. Continue to clock until 200 symbols have been produced (to mix initial data).

3. Keep c_t and c_{t-1} and load the last 128 generated bits into the four LFSRs.

In Figure 4.7 all bits are shifted in starting always with the *least significant bit* (LSB)[4] first; for example, from the third byte of the address, ADR[2], first ADR$_{16}$ is entered, followed by ADR$_{17}$, and so on. Finally, the last generated 128 bits denoted here conveniently by $Z[0], \ldots, Z[15]$ are fed back into the feedback registers as shown in Figure 4.8.

The incoming and outgoing payloads are treated separately and payload keys are generated for each of them. Figure 2.4 shows the timing of the encryption and decryption processes.

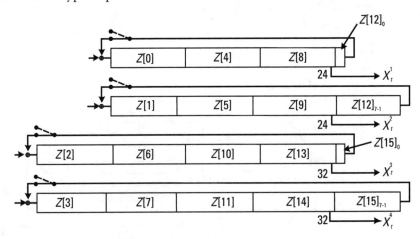

Figure 4.8 Second loading of the LFSRs with the payload key.

4. The LSB of $X[i]$ corresponds to bit $8i$ of the sequence X, and the most significant bit (MSB) of $X[i]$ to $8i + 7$.

4.5 Implementation aspects

When building a Bluetooth device, one has to decide how to implement the algorithms. A hardware implementation is the best alternative when speed and power consumption are important. Software implementations allow fast development and are flexible. In this section we discuss the implementation of SAFER+ and E_0. Since the authentication process and K_C derivation are not very time critical in most Bluetooth usage scenarios, a natural choice for SAFER+ is to implement it in software. Good software implementations can easily be found on various Web sites [14].

The implementation choice for E_0 is not that obvious. Since E_0 is always running when transmitting encrypted data, it is advantageous to implement E_0 in hardware on devices that should have very low power consumption. Because encryption takes place at the physical layer in the communication stack, a hardware implementation fits well together with an implementation where other low-layer functionality is realized in hardware. The design of E_0 allows for a further simplification that reduces the number of times one has to clock the four LFSRs. The reader might have observed the special structure of the feedback polynomials. These are so-called windmill polynomials, which have the property that one can construct a linear sequential machine that, provided it is correctly initialized, for each clock cycle generates four consecutive symbols of the sequence that the normal LFSR would generate (see also [15]).

The way a windmill construction works is best shown in Figure 4.9 using the example windmill polynomial $t^4 + t^3 + 1$. Shown first is a classical LFSR construction. The output at the third register element forms the maximum length, period 15 sequence starting with the symbols 00010011 . . . . Next is shown a windmill construction that generates the same sequence, but now three symbols for each tick of the clock.

It is now easy to see that the number of required clock cycles in a windmill realization of E_0 is only a quarter of that of a direct LFSR implementation.

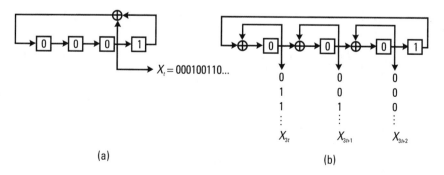

(a)   (b)

Figure 4.9 A windmill construction using windmill polynomial $t^4 + t^3 + 1$.

Hence it is possible to clock a windmill variant of E_0 only at one-fourth of the clock frequency of a variant with direct LFSRs. The lower clock frequency reduces power consumption in most very large scale intergration (VLSI) implementations. The windmill implementation is also feasible in software.

References

[1]   van Oorschot, P. C., A. J. Menezes, and S. A. Vanstone, *Handbook of Applied Cryptography*, Boca Raton, FL: CRC Press, 1997.

[2]   SAGE, *3GPP TS 35.201, the 3GPP Confidentiality and Integrity Algorithms; Document 1: f8 and f9 specifications, Version 5.0.0*, 3rd Generation Partnership Programme, 2002.

[3]   Massey, J. L., and R. A. Rueppel, "Method of, and Apparatus for, Transforming a Digital Sequence into an Encoded Form," U.S. Patent No. 4,797,922, 1989.

[4]   Rueppel, R. A., "Correlation Immunity and the Summation Combiner," *Advances in Cryptology, Crypto 85*, LNCS, Berlin: Springer-Verlag, 1986, pp. 260–272.

[5]   Meier, W., and O. Staffelbach, "Correlation Properties of Combiners with Memory in Stream Ciphers," *J. Cryptology*, Vol. 5, No. 1, 1992, pp. 67–86.

[6]   Golic, J. Dj., "Computation of Low-Weight Parity-Check Polynomials," *Electronic Letters*, Vol. 32, No. 21, October 1996, pp. 1981–1982.

[7]   Salmasizadeh, M., J. Dj. Golic, and E. Dawson, "Fast Correlation Attacks on the Summation Combiner," *J. Cryptology*, Vol. 13, No. 2, 2000, pp. 245–262.

[8]   Hermelin, M., and K. Nyberg, "Correlation Properties of the Bluetooth Summation Combiner," in J. Song, ed., *Proc. ICISC'99, 1999 International Conf. Information Security and Cryptography*, No. 1787 in LNCS, Berlin: Springer-Verlag, December 2000, pp. 17–29.

[9]   Knudsen, L. R., "A Detailed Analysis of Safer k," *J. Cryptology*, Vol. 13, No. 4, 2000, pp. 417–436.

[10] Kuregian, M., G. H. Khachatrian, and J. L. Massey, "Differential Cryptanalysis of Safer+," Technical Report, Cylink Corporation, Sunnyvale, CA, 20 April, 1999.

[11] ENS Ed, "Nessie Security Report," Technical Report Version 1.0, NESSIE Project, IST-2000-12324, 2002.

[12] Lidl, R., and H. Niederreiter, *Finite Fields, Encyclopedia of Mathematics and Its Applications*, Reading, MA: Addison-Wesley, 1983.

[13] Gill, A., *Linear Sequential Circuits: Analysis, Synthesis, and Applications*, New York: McGraw-Hill, 1966.

[14] Safer+ Development Kit, Available at http://us.cryptosoft.de/html/safer.htm, accessed November 2003.

[15] Smeets, B., and W. G. Chambers, "On Windmill pn-Sequence Generators," *IEE Proc-E*, Vol. 136, 1989, pp. 401–404.

5

Broadcast Encryption

Bluetooth has support for encrypted broadcast traffic. This is accomplished by distributing a common secret key to all slaves of the piconet. All broadcast traffic is then encrypted based on this common key. In version 1.1 [1] of the Bluetooth specification, details on broadcast encryption are somewhat vague at the LMP and HCI levels. In version 1.2 [2], efforts have been made to make the specified behavior unambiguous. Another change is that broadcast encryption has become an optional rather than mandatory feature. In this chapter we give an overview of the broadcast encryption mechanisms and the procedures used to enable encrypted broadcast traffic.

5.1   Overview

In order to support encrypted broadcast traffic, it is necessary for all slaves to have access to the same encryption/decryption key. For this purpose, a special link key has been defined to be used as a basis for the link encryption key. Since the piconet master issues this key, it is denoted by *master key*, K_{master}. The master key can only be used for one session; otherwise, devices that previously were members of a piconet governed by the same master could potentially listen in to the current conversation. Because of this, the master key is a *temporary key*.

One would think that once the master key has been distributed, a device can freely switch to the correct decryption key (which is based on the semipermanent key for individual traffic and on the master key for broadcast traffic) as needed. However, there is a practical problem with this approach. The receiver cannot determine whether to use the key for the master-slave connection or the key for the broadcast connection until the *LT_ADDR* is interpreted. If this address is all zeros, the message is a broadcast; otherwise it is destined to an individual device. Since the LT_ADDR is received rather close to the payload, there is very little time for the decryption machinery to get properly initialized before the deciphering starts. To avoid the uncertainty of which key to use, only one key can be valid at a time. As a consequence of this, there are three supported modes for traffic in Bluetooth:

1. No encryption—all traffic is in plain text.
2. Encryption on point-to-point links based on semipermanent link key[1] —broadcast traffic is still unencrypted.
3. Encryption on point-to-point and point-to-multipoint links—individual traffic and broadcast traffic are encrypted using the same encryption key.

The last case above implies that the link privacy is effectively removed with respect to all units sharing K_{master} but kept with respect to the rest of the world.

5.2   Preparing for broadcast encryption

In a broadcast scenario, since all slaves use the same encryption key, they must all support the encryption key length that the master chooses. Some countries have put export restrictions on hardware equipped with encryption circuitry. For this reason, the effective key length of the encryption key can be restricted to something less than 128 bits using the procedure described in Section 3.6.2. The maximum length supported is determined by the manufacturer and cannot be changed afterwards. In practice, this is accomplished by only implementing a subset of the key constraining polynomials defined in Table 3.2.

In order to select the key length, the master must know what lengths are supported for all individual members of the piconet. For devices compliant with version 1.1, there is no standardized way of obtaining this information, and the only available method is the key negotiation procedure that we described in Section 3.6.2. The complexity of gathering individual capabilities and negotiating the key size is one of the reasons broadcast encryption capability is a feature not always implemented in 1.1-compliant devices. Among the 1.1-compliant units that have this feature, practical tests have shown that interoperability between different manufacturers is not particularly good.

---

1. The 1.2 specification indicates that if a master key has been distributed, individual traffic can be encrypted based on that temporary key in this mode. As broadcast messages are unencrypted, the device is not forced to use K_{master} and the individual semipermanent keys give higher security.

The interoperability has been considerably improved in the 1.2 version of the specification [2] with the two new LMP commands:

- `LMP encryption key size mask req`
- `LMP encryption key size mask res`

The first command can be used by the master to request a bit mask that describes the supported key length (in bytes) by the slave. The slave uses the second command to return the supported key length (for the details; see Section 5.3). Furthermore, the *LMP features mask*, exchanged at link setup, defines what features are available in a device. From version 1.2, the number of possible features that can be defined have been increased significantly by the means of *extended* features masks. This is just a new LM PDU for which the bit positions in the payload refer to the extended features. Generally, for each optional LMP feature, the features mask indicates whether it is supported or not. As broadcast encryption is now defined to be an optional feature, it is supported only if the corresponding bit in the extended features mask is set. Legacy devices do not have the extended features mask, but it is possible for a new device to determine this from the LMP version number.

5.3   Switching to broadcast encryption

Before encrypted broadcast is possible, the master must change the current link key. To switch from the semipermanent to the temporary key, a few steps must be carried out. First, the master generates the temporary link key, K_{master}. Obviously, this key cannot be sent in plaintext. One option would be to distribute it over encrypted links. However, this imposes an unnecessary restriction, as it mandates an initial switch to encrypted master-slave traffic, even in cases where the application requesting broadcast traffic does not need it. Instead, the key is sent XORed with an overlay that is a function of the current link key and a public random number. The details of this scheme can be found in Section 3.4.5.

Whether or not broadcast encryption is supported can be determined via the LMP features mask. Furthermore, as we discussed previously, one can request the supported key lengths using the **LMP encryption key size mask req**. In this PDU, there are 16 bits whose positions correspond to the same length in bytes of the encryption key. For each supported length, the corresponding bit is set, and for each unsupported length, the bit is not set. Thus, the least significant bit corresponds to an 8-bit key, while the most significant bit corresponds to a 128-bit key. After acquiring this information from all slaves,

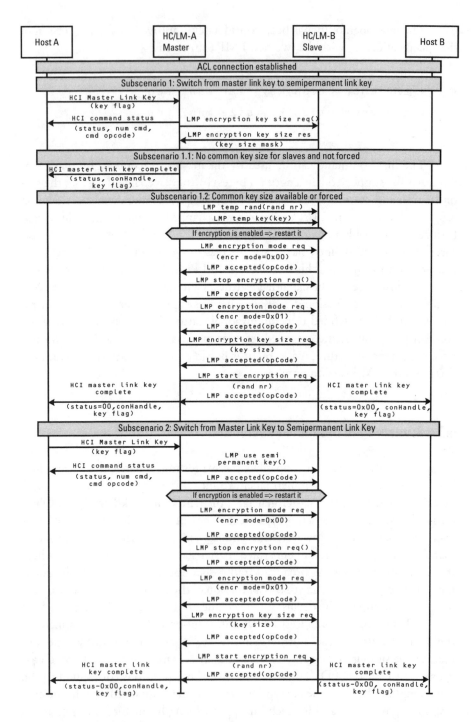

the master can decide which is the greatest co
request this to be used.

The *encryption mode* parameter of the LM
PDU determines whether to use encryption or
0x2, encryption applies to individually addresse
fic). Additionally, if a temporary link key is us
encrypted; if a semipermanent link key is use
encrypted. Note that setting the encryption mo
from version 1.2. The mode is still part of the s
backward compatibility with 1.1-compliant device

Consequently, the encryption mode para
`Write Encryption Mode` command can or
`0x1`.

Figure 5.1 depicts a message sequence chart
setting up broadcast encryption as well as returning fi
link encryption. For enabling of the master link key,
`Key` command with Key_Flag set to `0x01` is issued b

The same random number must be used i
`encryption req` commands; otherwise, differen
values will cause problems once encryption is switched
decide whether to attempt broadcasting encrypted data
set to receive encrypted broadcast data, but the recomme

If, for some rare necessary reason, the mutual authe
`LMP temp rand` and `LMP temp key` fails, the LM
issue the detach procedure for that link. This will allow th
even though one of the devices may be erroneous.

References

[1] Bluetooth Special Interest Group, *The Bluetooth Wireless Specificat*
     ary 2001.

[2] Bluetooth Special Interest Group, *Specification of the Bluetooth Sys*
     System Package, November 2003.

Figure 5.1 Message sequence chart for setting up broadcast encryption and for returning to individual link encryption.

6

Security Policies and Access Control

The security functionality defined in the Bluetooth baseband provides the system with the necessary building blocks for setting up a private radio link between devices. While this is a necessary component, it certainly is not enough to build a flexible security architecture upon. In one likely scenario of a Bluetooth-equipped laptop, a single Bluetooth radio link is shared by many different applications running on the host. Each of these may have completely different security requirements. For instance, some services may require authorization before a connection is allowed, while others are open to all incoming requests. Furthermore, confidentiality may or may not be an issue for a specific application, which suggests that encryption should be negotiable on the link. The Bluetooth SIG produced a white paper[1] [1] that outlines a possible architecture that addresses these issues. This white paper shows how to handle the requirements induced by security mode 2 (for the details on security mode 2, see Section 2.5.1). This chapter discusses the ideas and concepts presented in the white paper.

6.1 Objectives

A service may have particular requirements for authorization, authentication, and confidentiality. For the definitions of these terms, see Section 1.2.2. While these properties are not independent, it is desirable for the applications running

---

1. A *white paper* describes a preferred solution to a specific problem, but it is in no way mandated for compliance to the Bluetooth specification. Therefore, the security manager architecture described here may not be present in all existing Bluetooth products.

on the host to ask for specific settings regarding these properties on an individual basis. Clearly, the order in which services start cannot be known beforehand. A connection may start without any security switched on; then, at some point in time, a new service is initiated that asks for encryption. As this requires some LMP signaling over the link, some stack support is needed in order to effectuate the switch to encrypted mode. The goal of an access control mechanism is to provide means for the applications to request the type of connection they want. This is referred to as *service level–enforced* security. In particular, what is described below pertains to devices operating in security mode 2 (see Section 2.5.1 for a general discussion on different security modes).

6.1.1   Trust relations

In this context, a *trusted* device refers to a device to which a security relation has been established that is to last for more than the duration of the current session. Typically, personal devices that one would like to be able to hook up to more than once fall into this category, such as a headset and a mobile phone, a PDA that synchronizes to the desktop computer, or a mobile phone that is used for dial-up networking by a laptop computer. A trusted device is given unconditional access to all services running on the host after its identity has been confirmed through the authentication protocol.

For other user scenarios, the connection is of a more temporary nature. It is of interest to encrypt the link to have privacy, but a permanent bonding between the involved devices is not necessary, as this connection is not likely to be restored at a later time. It could also be the case that a fixed security relationship does exist, but the far-end device is not granted unrestricted access to services running on the near-end device. Such devices are referred to as *untrusted*.

A possible refinement of the trusted and untrusted relationships is to have these properties defined not per device but rather per service or group of services.

6.1.2   Security levels

A service can freely set its requirements on authorization, authentication, and encryption as long as the settings obey the basic rules of link level security. For instance, one cannot request encryption without authentication. From the possible access requirements, services fall within three security levels:

1. Authorization and authentication;
2. Authentication only;
3. Services open to all devices.

In case authorization is desired, the user must actively approve access to a service unless the connecting client runs on a trusted device (which automatically has access to all services running on a host). There are also authentication-only services, for which no authorization is necessary. Finally, the open services need neither authorization nor authentication. Obviously, the latter implies that the link level cannot be encrypted, as the protocol requires at least one authentication before the encrypted mode is possible.

6.1.3 Flexibility

In order to be usable, the security architecture must provide for individual settings of the access policies of different services. Opening up for one application shall not automatically also open for others. For instance, a cellular phone may have an open policy for accessing service discovery records and business card exchange but a restrictive policy for headset access and dial-up networking. In the same manner, for a service that has to deal with changing remote devices (such as file transfer and business card exchange), access granted to that service does not open for access to other services on the device, neither does it grant automatic future access to the service on the device.

In order to increase usability, the amount of user intervention to access a service should be kept at a minimum. Basically, it is needed when setting up a trusted relationship with a device or when allowing a limited access to a service.

6.1.4 Implementation considerations

In Bluetooth, protocol multiplexing can take place at and above the L2CAP layer. The higher layer multiplexing protocols (i.e., above L2CAP) are in some cases Bluetooth specific (e.g., RFCOMM) and in other cases nonunique for Bluetooth (e.g., OBEX). Some protocols even have their own security features. The security architecture must account for this in that different protocols may enforce the security policies for different services. For instance, L2CAP enforces security for cordless telephony, RFCOMM enforces security for dial-up networking, and OBEX enforces its security policy for file transfer and synchronization.

Lower layers need not know about security settings and policies at higher layers. Furthermore, security policies may differ for the client and server role of a particular service. That implies that peers may enforce different security policies for the same service due to their different roles. This also must be handled by the security manager.

6.2   Security manager architecture

This section will describe an architecture that fulfills the objectives set forth in the previous sections.

6.2.1   Overview

A security manager architecture working along the lines discussed so far is depicted in Figure 6.1. The main tasks it has to accomplish consist of:

- Store security-related information for services;
- Store security-related information for devices;
- Accept or reject access requests by protocols or applications;
- When required, enforce authentication/encryption before connecting to the application;

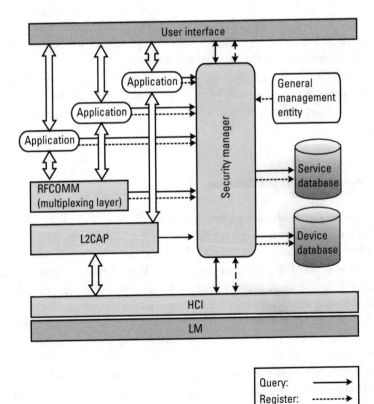

Figure 6.1 The proposed security manager architecture.

- Initiate the setup of trusted relationships on device level;
- Query the user or an application for pass-keys when needed.

The security manager architecture offloads from applications the burden of implementing all these details themselves. A well-defined and consistent link level security policy is automatically available for all applications utilizing Bluetooth connectivity. The protocol to interface with the security manager consists of simple query/response and registration procedures. As the security policy is encapsulated within the security manager, modifications to this can take place without the need for updating the entities that interact with it. This structure also means that legacy applications without inherent support for direct communication with the security manager can benefit from device access control via the multiplexing layer (e.g., RFCOMM) and L2CAP. One can notice that security policies apply to inbound as well as outbound traffic. It is quite natural that incoming requests need adequate permissions before they are accepted. However, if a user has requested a specific application to run over an encrypted link, the security manager should also make sure that the encryption is switched on before such a connection request is sent to a remote device. The application running locally cannot know for sure if the remote device has applied the same security requirements for this application. Consequently, the security manager will enforce encryption just to be certain that a more relaxed setting at the remote end will not override the local settings.

6.2.2 Device trust level

From the security manager's point of view, each remote device connecting to it falls within one of three defined device trust levels:

1. *Trusted device:* A previously authenticated device for which a link key is stored and which is labeled *trusted* in the device database.
2. *Untrusted device:* A previously authenticated device for which a link key is stored but which is labeled *untrusted* in the device database.
3. *Unknown device:* No security information is available for this device. By definition this device is untrusted.

The security manager will maintain a device database (see Section 6.2.5) of all known devices and act according to the policy for the trust level of the remote device and the service it tries to connect to. A trusted relationship is usually established during the pairing procedure. The user can be notified and given the option to add the remote device to the list of trusted devices. It is also possible to add untrusted devices later on when they are being granted access to a service requiring authorization running on the local host. Again, the user will be notified and asked if the remote device should change status from untrusted to trusted. Whenever a remote device has an associated link key, authentication is performed according to the procedure specified in the LMP and baseband specification. To be verified as trusted, the authentication must succeed and the trusted flag must be set in the internal database. For unknown devices, a pairing is necessary before authentication can take place.

6.2.3   Security level for services

Analogously to the case of a device database, the security manager has a service database for settings related to specific services rather than devices. The security level of a service is defined by three attributes:

1. *Authorization required:* Trusted devices are automatically granted access, while untrusted devices need user-assisted authorization before an access right is granted. Authorization requires authentication in order to verify the claimed identity of the remote device.

2. *Authentication required:* The remote device must be authenticated before access to the application is granted.

3. *Encryption required:* The link must be switched to encrypted mode before access to the service or application is granted.

These attributes can be set independently for incoming and outgoing connections. By definition, each service must be handled by some application. It is the responsibility of each application to register with the security manager and define its security level. To be more precise, the application itself is not required to do this—some other entity may do it on behalf of the application (such as the entity responsible for setting the path in the Bluetooth protocol stack). Not only do applications need to register, but multiplexing protocols above L2CAP must also do this.

If no service database record exists for a particular incoming or outgoing connection request, the following default settings apply:

- *Incoming connection:* Authorization (thus, implicitly also authentication) required.

- *Outgoing connection:* Authentication required.

6.2.4   Connection setup

In the following we will differentiate between *channel establishment* and *connection establishment.* The former is defined as creating an L2CAP channel, that is, the logical connection between two end points in peer devices at the L2CAP level, characterized by their respective *channel identifiers* (CID). The L2CAP channel is serving a single application or higher layer protocol. The connection establishment is defined as a connection between two peer applications or higher layer protocols mapped onto a channel. The decision on what security measures to enforce is taken after determining the security level of the requested service. This will minimize unnecessary user interaction, as authentications and authorizations can be initiated on a strictly as-needed basis. It also implies that authentication cannot take place when the ACL link is established, but rather when the request to a service is submitted.

Generally, the flow for an (accepted) incoming L2CAP channel establishment is as follows (depicted in Figure 6.2):

1. Connection makes request to L2CAP;
2. L2CAP requests access from the security manager;
3. The security manager looks up the security policy for the requested service in the service database;
4. The security manager looks up the security policy for the connecting device in the device database;
5. If necessary, the security manager enforces authentication and encryption;
6. The security manager grants access to the service;
7. L2CAP continues to establish the connection.

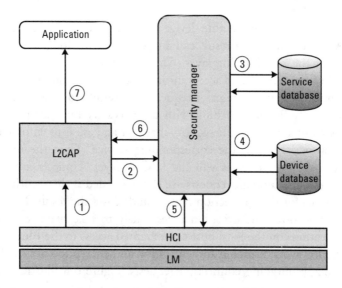

Figure 6.2 Access control procedure for L2CAP channel establishment.

For incoming connection requests, the access control may end up being duplicated. First, the L2CAP layer will query the security manager. The query contains a parameter identifying which protocol submitted the query and the *BD_ADDR* of the remote device. Based on this information, the security manager decides whether to grant or refuse the connection and if there is a need to enforce authentication and encryption. Should this be the case, the security manager will make sure this is carried out before it grants access to the submitted request. The simplest way to achieve this for the security manager is by interfacing to the lower Bluetooth layers through designated HCI link control commands. Of course, this is only possible if the HCI is present in the device implementation, but in any case some means of equivalent functionality must be available. For some submitted requests, the user may be asked to authorize the connection.

In addition to this, the multiplexing protocol above L2CAP (e.g., RFCOMM) may also do an access control query. The protocol handling entity will query the security manager with all the available multiplexing information (including protocol identification for the submitter and corresponding channel identifications associated with that particular protocol) it received with the connection request. As is the case for L2CAP queries, the security manager will make a decision whether the request is granted or not based on the registered security policy settings for the protocol and remote device in question, and inform the protocol handling entity of the result.

Clearly, the duplicated security manager requests may lead to repeated authentication events, causing unnecessary signaling over the air or repeated authorization requests requiring user interaction. To avoid this, the security manager should store a temporary value concerning the status of the request. If an authentication with the remote device has been successful when triggered by the L2CAP interaction, the result can simply be reused for the second query originating at the multiplexing layer. The same holds for connection request that have already been granted access through the authorization process.

Duplicate (or even triplicate) requests can result from outgoing connection requests as well. First, if built with the necessary means, the application itself may submit a query to the security manager and ask it to enforce the security policy associated with the corresponding service. Then the multiplexing protocol will do the same, as will the L2CAP layer. Unnecessary actions in response to these redundant requests are easily avoided if the security manager tracks the status for the connection request and reuses the result. Naturally, for outgoing connections authorization is less likely to take place, as one would expect applications on the local host to be granted access to the Bluetooth radio by default. However, enforcing authentication and encryption are valid requirements for many outgoing connection requests. Figure 6.3 illustrates how the redundant security manager queries are generated for incoming and outgoing connections, respectively.

6.2.5 Database contents and registration procedure

There are two databases maintained by the security manager—the *device database* and the *service database*. Each record of the device database contains information regarding device identity, trust level, and link key shared with the particular unit. It may also be useful to store other information, such as a human-readable device name for simpler user interaction upon authorization requests. To be useful over several sessions, the database should be stored in nonvolatile memory.

The service database contains information regarding the security level (i.e., authorization, authentication, and encryption requirements) for incoming and outgoing requests. Furthermore, a *protocol/service multiplexor* (PSM) value is stored. The PSM value is used by the L2CAP layer during channel establishment to route the connection request to the right upper layer (several higher layer protocols can be multiplexed over L2CAP). Whenever L2CAP submits a

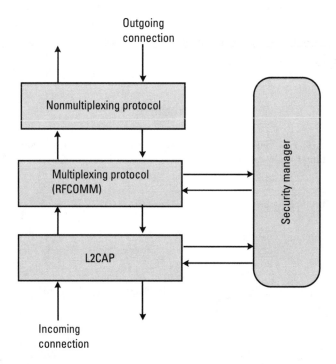

Figure 6.3 Duplicate security manager requests following incoming and outgoing connection requests.

request, the service manager will use the PSM value to identify which higher layer protocol a connection request belongs to. With this information available, the correct security policy settings can be applied to the connection request. More information may also be stored, such as a human-readable service name. The service database can store its information in nonvolatile memory, or it is required that services register at every boot instance.

The service manager is responsible for maintaining the device database. It must be updated every time that a bonding with a device takes place. For new devices, a new record is generated. If existing link keys are changed, the device database must be updated accordingly. Changing the trust level of a device (untrusted to trusted or vice versa) must be reflected in the database. Should the local device be set into security mode 3 (i.e., *link level–enforced* security), it is possible to utilize the security manager for this also. Then, in order to avoid untrusted devices getting unwanted access to local services, the security manager should remove all existing link keys for untrusted devices.

Security information pertaining to services or applications need to be registered with the security manager for inclusion in the service database before a service is accessed. This can be done by the applications themselves or by designated security delegates. Registration includes security levels for incoming and outgoing requests, protocol identification, and the PSM used at the L2CAP layer. Additionally, multiplexing protocols such as RFCOMM also need to register with the security manager.

Reference

[1]   Müller, T., ed., "Bluetooth Security Architecture," White Paper Revision 1.0, Bluetooth Special Interest Group, July 1999.

7

Attacks, Strengths, and Weaknesses

Until now we have gone through many details of the mechanisms in Bluetooth that aim to provide means for secure data transmission. It is now appropriate to investigate what the overall result is. Assessing the security of a communication system is a difficult task and encompasses many aspects. It would take us too far to pursue a complete review of the security aspects of using Bluetooth. Instead, we limit ourselves to a review of the strengths and weaknesses of the security mechanisms defined in Bluetooth. In particular, we discuss how existing weaknesses can be exploited to attack communicating Bluetooth devices. The weaknesses can be used to mount various kinds of attacks. For example, attacks that attempt to eavesdrop on the data that the Bluetooth devices send to each other or to manipulate (modify) this data. Another attack that we discuss is more in the realm of traffic analysis and reveals, among other things, the location of the Bluetooth device (owner). For a broader overview of the security of Bluetooth and the 802.11 wireless systems, we refer to [1].

7.1 Eavesdropping

When a Bluetooth connection is set up without activating the link encryption, it is obvious that such a connection is easily eavesdropped on. Furthermore, it is fairly easy for an attacker to substitute payload data with other payload data. When activating link encryption between two units, the communicating units cause the data sent via the link to not be accessible to outsiders. One may be tempted to believe that when encryption is activated, the above mentioned substitution manipulation is also blocked. However, this is not true, as we will see in the next section. There we show that by carefully manipulating the data and the corresponding CRC data, it is possible to make the receiver accept manipulated payload data. Thus, what remains to be investigated in more detail is the question of how good the cipher itself is, and how easy it is to break the encryption method. This will be the subject of the remainder of this section.

It is common practice to assume that the attacker knows the bits of the stream that the ciphering engine has produced. The question that one wants to solve is whether it is possible to recover the ciphering key. It follows from the construction of E_0 that this requires two steps: first the attack must provide the payload key; subsequently from one or possibly several recovered payload keys, one has to determine the value of the constraint key K'_C. When K'_C is determined, the eavesdropper can eavesdrop on the communication between two units. This will be the case until the units execute a new mutual authentication or until the two units perform an explicit update of K'_C through the operations described in Section 3.6.1. For simplicity we assume that the value of K'_C is constant during the time the eavesdropper wants to attack. For the same reason we assume the eavesdropper has access to the plaintext as long as the cryptanalysis is performed that leads to the recovery of K_P. The important parameter is how long it takes for the eavesdropper to determine K_P in this setup. This will give a lower limit on the amount of time needed to find K'_C. The actual time needed to determine K'_C will be larger, as one may have to work back from one or several KP to recover K'_C.

Since the Bluetooth specification was released, researchers have presented their analysis of and attacks on E_0. Attacks on E_0 are known that have work (time) complexity that is essentially less than $O(2^{128})$, which is less than the exhaustive search through the key space. General ideas to find weaknesses in the combining functions can be found in [2]. Here we report only on two, more specialized, attacks. Each attack illustrates different approaches to promising breaks of E_0. In these works, the main idea is to use the correlation and/or the algebraic structure that exists between the output bits and the input bits.

Correlation attacks were pioneered by Siegenthaler in the mid-1980s. They were made effective on a large class of stream cipher generators by the ideas of Meier and Staffelbach in a series of publications starting with [3], of which [4] is particularly relevant to E_0. The E_0 construction tries to lower the correlations this attack can utilize. In [5], Hermelin and Nyberg show that there exists a useful correlation between the stream cipher outputs z_t and the stream bits $v_t = x_{1t} \oplus x_{2t} \oplus x_{3t} \oplus x_{4t}$. See Figure 4.6. The latter sequence is the sequence that is generated by a fictive LFSR with feedback polynomial $g(t) = f_1(t)f_2(t)f_3(t)f_4(t)$, that is, the product of the four feedback polynomials of the four LFSRs in E_0. The polynomial $g(t)$ is of degree 128. A successful correlation attack provides the attacker with the initial state of this fictive LFSR. It is then a simple matter to solve a small set of linear equations, in 128 unknown variables, to compute the initial states of each of the four LFSRs in the original E_0.

Before we can proceed, we need the following definition and some extra notations.

Definition 1.   *Let f, g be two Boolean functions in n variables. The correlation between f and g is the value*

$$C(f,g) = \frac{\#\{x \in B_2^n ; f(x) = g(x)\} - \#\{x \in B_2^n ; f(x) \neq g(x)\}}{2^n} \quad (7.1)$$

where B_2^n is the n-dimensional vector space over $B_2 = \{0, 1\}$.

We are looking for correlations to linear functions. If $x \in B_2^n$ is an n-dimensional variable and $w \in B_2^n$ an n-dimensional constant, then we can define the linear function

$$L_w(x) = \bigoplus_{i=1}^{n} w_i x_i \quad (7.2)$$

and study the correlation value

$$C(f, L_w) \quad (7.3)$$

for different values of w. We are interested in finding the value(s) of w that maximize $|C(f, L_w)|$. This is the basic idea. Applying this to Bluetooth is not directly straightforward. Yet some correlation between input bits and output bits must remain. Omitting the details, Hermelin and Nyberg derived that

$$C\left(z_t \oplus z_{t-1} \oplus z_{t-3}, v_t \oplus v_{t-1} \oplus v_{t-3}\right) = -\frac{1}{16}$$

The correlation value $-1/16$ is lower (in absolute value) than the corresponding value for the original summation combiner by [6], due to the IIR filtering induced by (4.31). However, the value could have been even reduced to $C = 1/64$ when the linear mappings were changed in (4.31). The latter was observed by Hermelin and Nyberg [5].

Instead of attacking the four LFSRs simultaneously, one can attack, say, only three and assume the remaining one to have a known state. The attack then proceeds by attacking the three LFSRs for each possible known (trial) state. This is referred to as a *guess-and-divide attack*. The obtained correlation, together with a guess-and-divide attack setup in which the attacker guesses the content of one LFSR, gives an effective attack (in complexity). This attack, described in detail in [7], can recover the initial state of E_0 in

$$2^{68} \text{ operations using } 2^{43} \text{ observed/known symbols}$$

Because the required number of observed/known symbols is much larger than the number of symbols in a payload frame, this attack does not lead to a direct attack that reveals the link key. A more powerful attack in terms of the required number of symbols was pioneered by Krause [8], which gives an attack with

$$2^{77} \text{ time effort using only 128 observed/known symbols}$$

This attack is particular interesting[1] because it can be used to find K'_C from K_P. The latter result also clearly shows that it is not appropriate to use the modified summation combiner right away, and as we have seen, Bluetooth uses an additional key loading step and restarts the encryption engine for each frame. The recent, improved correlation attack by Golic et al. [9] achieves

$$2^{70} \text{ time effort using less than 1 frame of observed/known symbols}$$

Finally, we also mention the result by Ekdahl and Johansson [10, 11], where a correlation type attack is given that achieves

$$2^{63} \text{ time effort using } 2^{34} \text{ bits observed/known symbols}$$

Hence, again a better (lower) complexity was obtained at the expense of having to use a long (much longer) observed sequence. A very important ingredient in the correlation attack is formed by the linear equations that are used to find the initial state of the registers under attack. Recently, based on techniques stemming from attacks on other encryption mechanisms, a new set of attacks have been devised that use the fact that in certain (stream) ciphers one can exploit that one can solve systems of nonlinear equations (with terms of not too high a degree). For E_0 we expect the relations between the input bits and output bits to not have too high a degree. This follows partly from the fact that the rather simple feedback scheme and the combining structure will only give rise to a "moderate" explosion in high-order terms in the equations that describe the output bits in terms of the initial state. The works by Armknecht [12, 13] and recently by Courtois [14] show the power of this kind of approach. For example,

---

1. Although the space complexity is $O(2^{77})$.

Armknecht discovered a system of nonlinear equations with a degree of at most 4. The system can be transformed through linearization into a system of linear equations with about 2^{24} unknowns.

We follow Armknecht [12, 14] to explain some of the steps of the attack. We refer to [12, 14] for the details. The idea is to consider multivariate relations between output and input bits, that is, relations of output and input bits using nonlinear expressions. That we have a combiner with memory in the cipher complicates matters, but provided the number of states induced by the memory is small, the multivariate relations that can be found are useful. For Bluetooth, we recall that the combiner has memory 4; that is, we have 216 states. Armknecht and Krause have proven that for any combiner with k inputs and l bits of memory, the required multivariate relations always exist and have a degree of at most $\lceil k(l + 1)/2 \rceil$. For E_0, this number is thus $\lceil 4(4 + 1)/2 \rceil = 10$. Hence, Armknecht's direct investigation leads to a substantially better set of relations. We show how Armknecht cleverly obtained his set of nonlinear equations of degree 4.

Recall that at time t the output z_t is produced and that two new memory bits $(Q_t, P_t) = \mathbf{c}_t$ are computed. This is done by the following equations:

$$z_t = x_{1t} \oplus x_{2t} \oplus x_{3t} \oplus x_{4t} \oplus P_t \tag{7.4}$$

$$P_{t+1} = \prod\nolimits_2(t) \oplus \prod\nolimits_1(t) \oplus P_t \oplus P_t \oplus P_{t-1} \oplus Q_t \oplus Q_{t-1} \tag{7.5}$$

$$Q_{t+1} = \prod\nolimits_4(t) \oplus \prod\nolimits_3(t)P_t \oplus P_{t-1} \oplus \prod\nolimits_2(t)Q_t \prod\nolimits_1(t)P_t Q_t \oplus Q_t \tag{7.6}$$

where the $\prod_k(t)$ are functions in the variables $\{x_{1t}, x_{2t}, x_{3t}, x_{4t}\}$ by taking the XOR sum over all possible products of distinct terms of degree k. The $\prod_k(t)$ are thus the XOR sum of monomials of degree k:

$$\prod\nolimits_1(t) = x_{1t} \oplus x_{2t} \oplus x_{3t} \oplus x_{4t}$$

$$\prod\nolimits_2(t) = x_{1t}x_{2t} \oplus x_{1t}x_{3t} \oplus x_{1t}x_{4t} \oplus x_{2t}x_{3t} \oplus x_{2t}x_{4t} \oplus x_{3t}x_{4t}$$

$$\prod\nolimits_3(t) = x_{1t}x_{2t}x_{3t} \oplus x_{1t}x_{2t}x_{4t} \oplus x_{1t}x_{3t}x_{4t} \oplus x_{2t}x_{3t}x_{4t}$$

$$\prod\nolimits_4(t) = x_{1t}x_{2t}x_{3t}x_{4t}$$

Following Armknecht, we introduce now two sets of variables:

$$A(t) = \prod\nolimits_4(t) \oplus \prod\nolimits_3(t)P_t \oplus P_{t-1}$$

$$B(t) = \prod\nolimits_2(t) \oplus \prod\nolimits_1(t)P_t \oplus 1$$

which allow us to write a more compact expression for P and Q:

$$P_{t+1} = B(t) \oplus 1 \oplus P_{t-1} \oplus P_t \oplus Q_t \oplus Q_{t-1} \qquad (7.7)$$

$$Q_{t+1} = A(t) \oplus B(t)Q_t \qquad (7.8)$$

By multiplying (7.8) with $B(t)$ and arranging terms and using the fact that for Boolean variables $x^2 = x$, we get

$$0 = B(t)\big(A(t) \oplus Q_t \oplus Q_{t+1}\big) \qquad (7.9)$$

Equation (7.7) is equivalent to

$$Q_t \oplus Q_{t-1} = B(t) \oplus 1 \oplus P_{t-1} \oplus P_t \oplus P_{t+1} \qquad (7.10)$$

By inserting (7.10) into (7.9) with index $t+1$ instead of t, we get

$$0 = B(t)\big(A(t) \oplus B(t+1) \oplus 1 \oplus P_t \oplus P_{t+1} \oplus P_{t+2}\big)$$

Using (7.4), we eliminate all memory bits in the equation and get the following equation, which holds for every time instant t,

$$
\begin{aligned}
0 = {} & 1 \oplus z_{t-1} \oplus z_t \oplus z_{t+1} \oplus z_{t+2} \\
& \oplus \textstyle\prod_1(t)(z_t z_{t+2} \oplus z_t z_{t+1} \oplus z_t z_{t-1} \oplus z_{t+2} \oplus z_{t+1} \oplus z_{t-1} \oplus 1) \\
& \oplus \textstyle\prod_2(t)(1 \oplus z_{t-1} \oplus z_t \oplus z_{t+1} \oplus z_{t+2}) \\
& \oplus \textstyle\prod_3(t)z_t \oplus \textstyle\prod_4(t) \\
& \oplus \textstyle\prod_1(t-1) \oplus \textstyle\prod_1(t-1)\textstyle\prod_1(t)(1 \oplus z_t) \oplus \textstyle\prod_1(t-1)\textstyle\prod_2(t) \\
& \oplus \textstyle\prod_1(t+1)z_{t+1} \oplus \textstyle\prod_1(t+1)\textstyle\prod_1(t)z_{t+1}(1 \oplus z_t) \oplus \textstyle\prod_1(t+1)\textstyle\prod_2(t)z_{t+1} \\
& \oplus \textstyle\prod_2(t+1) \oplus \textstyle\prod_2(t+1)\textstyle\prod_1(t)(1 \oplus z_t) \oplus \textstyle\prod_2(t+1)\textstyle\prod_2(t) \\
& \oplus \textstyle\prod_1(t+2) \oplus \textstyle\prod_1(t+2)\textstyle\prod_1(t)(1 \oplus z_t) \oplus \textstyle\prod_1(t+2)\textstyle\prod_2(t)
\end{aligned}
$$

By inspection we easily see that this equation has terms of degree of at most 4 in the variables $\{x_{1t}, x_{2t}, x_{3t}, x_{4t}\}$. As the equation holds for any t, we get for every t a new equation. By iterating this, we can build a system of nonlinear equations with terms of degree of at most 4. Since the output bits $\{x_{1t}, x_{2t}, x_{3t}, x_{4t}\}$ stem from the four LFSRs and thus can be expressed as linear combinations of the initial state bits, we can rewrite the above equation in terms of the initial state bits $S_0 = \{s_0, s_1, \ldots, s_{127}\}$ and get

$$R\left(s_0, s_1, \ldots, s_{127}, z_0, z_1, \ldots, z_3\right) = 0$$

where R is a multivariate relation of degree of at most 4. The just-mentioned linearity allows us to write

$$S_1 = \mathcal{L}\left(s_0, s_1, \ldots, s_{127}\right) = \mathcal{L}(S_0)$$
$$S_2 = \mathcal{L}\left(s_1, s_2, \ldots, s_{128}\right) = \mathcal{L}\left(\mathcal{L}\left(s_0, s_1, \ldots, s_{127}\right)\right) = \mathcal{L}^2(S_0) \quad (7.11)$$
$$\vdots$$
$$S_t = \mathcal{L}\left(s_{t-1}, s_1, \ldots, s_{t+126}\right) = \mathcal{L}^t(S_0)$$

where $\mathcal{L}$ is the linear mapping that maps the state S_t to the state S_{t+1}. Because of this linearity, (7.11) will apply to all blocks of four consecutive output bits, that is,

$$R\left\{\left[\mathcal{L}^t(S_0)\right]_0, \left[\mathcal{L}^t(S_0)\right]_1, \ldots, \left[\mathcal{L}^t(S_0)\right]_{127}, z_t, \ldots, z_{t+3}\right\} = 0, \quad t = 0, 1, 2, \ldots$$

Here, by definition, $[\mathcal{L}^t(S_0)]_i = s_{t+i}$ for $i = 0, 1, \ldots, 127$. Thus we can write down relations between the 128 initial bit values and blocks of output symbols.

Another effect of the fact that the output bits $\{x_{1t}, x_{2t}, x_{3t}, x_{4t}\}$ can be expressed as a linear combination of the initial state bits is that as we build the system of relations, the number of distinct terms that will occur must have an upper limit, as there will be only a finite number of different terms that can occur. Indeed, Armknecht found that one has the upper bound $T = 17,440,047 \approx 2^{24.056}$.

The number T is important, as one has to clock at least that many times to get enough equations to solve the system of nonlinear equations through so-called linearization [15]. Strictly speaking, we do not know if we get enough independent equations, but experimental evidence shows that we expect the required number of times we have to clock to be in the neighborhood of T. The complexity to solve such a system by the Strassen algorithm is $7T^{\log_2 7}$. On a 64-bit machine, this can be reduced to $\frac{7}{64}T^{\log_2 7}$. There exists faster algorithms to solve nonlinear equations. In theory, one can solve a system in T^ω, $\omega \leq 2.376$ steps [16]. The complexity estimate from the Strassen algorithm is currently more realistic. Another algorithm that can be adopted for this is the XL algorithm [15]. The XL algorithm may work with less than T relations to start with.

We now briefly describe how the attack may be carried out after we have obtained the system of equations.

- We collect key stream bits and plug them into the equations.

- Say we have T key stream bits. There are about T monomials of degree ≤ 4 in the $n = 128$ variables. We consider each of these monomials as a new variable X_i. Suppose we have enough key stream bits and then obtain $M \geq T$ linear equations in T variables X_i that can be solved, say, by the method in [16] in complexity T^ω.

- Alternatively, especially when we have too few key stream bits, we may apply the XL algorithm [15, 17].

The value of T is thus crucial, and an attacker wants it to be as small as possible. However, for this we should have a lower degree in the monomials. Currently, one does not know how to find such an equation. However, recently Courtois [14] pushed the algebraic approach further by observing that one can utilize the fact that we can multiply the multivariate polynomial by another multivariate polynomial such that the product is of degree 3 in the initial state bit variables.

The main work load of the attack in [14] is for Bluetooth $O\left(\left[\binom{n}{4}\binom{n}{3} + \binom{n}{3}\right]^\omega\right)$. The complexity of the attack by Courtois is thus $O(2^{49})$. The attack requires $2^{23.4}$ output bits. Note that 2^{49} operations can be performed in about 35 hours on a 4-GHz machine. One should, however, be aware that in the complexity estimate there may be a large constant. In any case, the result by Courtois shows that the core in E_0 is not cryptographically strong.

Returning to E_0, we see that to obtain an actual attack that recovers K'_C, we have two options: (1) make the algebraic attack work with only 2,744 output bits[2], or (2) find a way to utilize that there exists a relation between the consecutive blocks of 2,744 output bits. The first option still exists, but it should require that we find equations of type (7.11) with degree less than 4. Currently, this has not been done. The second option is a result of the fact that the output blocks are generated with the same constraint key K'_C, BD_ADDR, and $RAND$ values, but different clock timer value. See Section 3.6.3. This is not infeasible, because the relation between the initial state values (where only the clock timer values differ) satisfies a linear relation over the finite field GF(2). Hence, we could rewrite our relations in terms of a specific initial state (say, with all clock bits

---

2. 2,744 is the maximum number of known plaintext bits encrypted with the same K_P.

equal to zero), the clock bits, and output bits.[3] We are not aware of any attacks that exploit this, nor do we have complexity estimates for such an attack.

We conclude that currently there is no attack known that breaks the complete encryption procedure with reasonable effort. However, the security margin is insufficient to feel comfortable about the years to come. Therefore, a stronger encryption alternative in Bluetooth would be welcome as a backup solution in case future attacks succeed to reduce the cryptanalytic workload to a practical level. Such future attacks may well exploit the fact that the output bits can be expressed approximately (probabilistically) with an algebraic relation in terms of the initial state bits with a lower degree than the exact (deterministic) relation. This is a continuation of the work of Armknecht and Courtois that we discussed.

7.2 Impersonation

In the previous section, the main concern was the confidentiality of the data that two units exchange. Another concern is that receivers want to be sure that they indeed receive data from the original sending party identified through the Bluetooth authentication procedure. An attacker has mainly two options:

1. Impersonate the original sending (or receiving) unit;
2. Insert/replace data (payloads) that is sent.

The first option requires the attacker to provide the correct response on the authentication challenge by the receiving unit. Currently, no attack on the SAFER+-based E_1 is known that achieves this within any realistic computational effort. Hence, the only realistic way to send wrong data to the receiver is by inserting/replacing data that is sent from the sending unit to the receiving unit. When no encryption is activated, this can easily be achieved by correctly setting the CRC check data in the payload after the data in the payload has been modified. This is indeed an easy task because the attacker knows the data bits that have been set/modified by the attacker and knows how to perform the CRC computation for the payload. When ciphering is activated, the same attack applies because the ciphering consists of adding (modulo 2) the bits of the key stream to the data. This is a linear operation, and since the CRC calculation is a linear operation too, the attacker can compute how to modify the CRC to make it agree with modifications in the encrypted data bits. Thus, the CRC mechanism combined with activated encryption is capable of detecting a modification

---

3. We use the fact that we can write the affine equation $S_t(C) = \mathcal{L}(S_0) + H(C)$ for fixed C, where H is a linear transformation and C the vector of 26 clock bits.

of the data sent only under the assumption that the attacker either not changes the CRC bits at all or only changes them more or less randomly. Figure 7.1 shows the principle of this attack.

Even when making random changes in the payload without correcting the CRC, an attacker has a chance to get the modified payload through. Assuming that we have random changes in the payload, the probability of success is 2^{-16}, which is not very small. However, this occurs for every payload packet, and the receiver would in this case be able to notice a very poor throughput due to a large portion of invalid incoming packets during the time the attack is conducted.

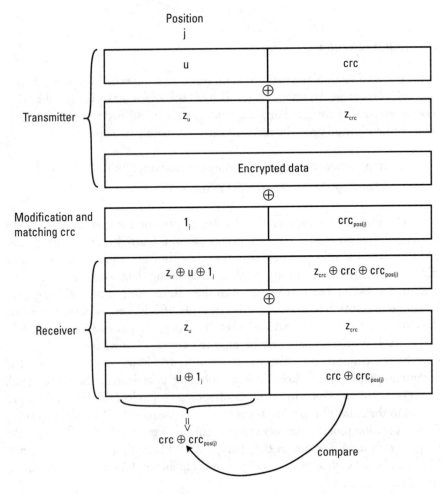

Figure 7.1 Substitution attack on encrypted data where at data position j the bit value is flipped.

Concluding, we see that the payload data in the Bluetooth 1.1 system is easily tampered with. Yet, in a practical system were encryption is activated, it is not at all easy to make something useful of this attack beyond the point of just disrupting the communication.[4] The attacker must somehow know the context of the payload data to conduct changes that are meaningful or effective. This is because some payload data is most likely intended for service operation in the higher layers of the communication stack, and other data is actual end-user/application data. Without knowing what data is sent, it is unlikely that the attacker achieves a particular desired change in the end-user data. Here Bluetooth benefits from the fact that encryption is performed at a very low level in the communication stack.

7.3 Pairing

The Bluetooth 1.1 specification is sensitive to passive and active attacks on the pairing procedure. The attacks only work if the attacker is present at the pairing occasion, which typically only occurs once between one pair of devices. Anyway, if pairing is performed in public places during a connection to an access point, point-of-sale machine, or printer, this can indeed be a dangerous threat. In this section we describe how a passive or active attack against the pairing works. In order to simplify the description, we only describe the combination key case. However, the attack can easily be generalized to the unit key pairing case. On the other hand, unit keys have other specific security issues. These issues will be discussed in Section 7.5.

The Bluetooth combination key is calculated as shown in Figure 3.3. In the figure, K denotes the current link key. In the pairing procedure, the current link is the initialization key K_{INIT}, which is derived as the output of the algorithm E_{22}. E_{22} takes as input the address of one of the Bluetooth units, BD_ADDR_A, a random value, IN_RAND, and the secret pass-key, that is,

$$K_{INIT} = E_{22}(BD\_ADDR\_A, IN\_RAND, PKEY)$$

The random value, IN_RAND, is sent in cleartext from unit B to unit A over the Bluetooth radio channel.

As shown in Figure 3.3, the initialization key is then used to encrypt random values, LK_RAND_A, and LK_RAND_B, which are used to derive the combination key K_{AB} (a similar procedure is used to exchange a unit key, as was shown in Chapter 3). A third part, or a "man in the middle," who observes all the

---

4. If disrupting the communication is a goal of the attacker, there are simpler ways to set up an attack.

communication between A and B during the pairing procedure obtains all parameters exchanged over the air interface. The parameters needed for an attack are the device address of A, BD_ADDR_A; the device address of B, BD_ADDR_B; the random value, IN_RAND; and the encrypted random values, $K_{INIT} \oplus LK\_RAND_A$ and $K_{INIT} \oplus LK\_RAND_A$. Hence, as is shown in Figure 3.3, the only unknown parameter used in the calculations of K_{AB}, is the pass-key. Given that attackers observe all these values, they might then try to guess which pass-key value that was used during the pairing. Each pass-key value then corresponds to a unique link key value. However, in order to check if the guess is correct, the attackers must have some additional information. This information is obtained if they also observe the authentication message exchange that always follows the link key calculation exchanges. At the authenticating procedure, the verifier sends a random value, AU_RAND, to the claimant unit. The claimant then sends a response, $SRES = E_2(BD\_ADDR\_claimant, AU\_RAND, K_{AB})$, where E_2 is the Bluetooth authentication algorithm. In summary, the attacker can observe the following parameters during the pairing procedure:

$A1 = IN\_RAND$

$A2 = K_{INIT} \oplus LK\_RAND\_A$

$A3 = K_{INIT} \oplus LK\_RAND\_B$

$A4 = AU\_RAND$

$A5 = SRES$

Using these observations, the attacker can guess the pass-key value $PKEY'$ and calculates the corresponding link key, K'_{AB}, as is shown in Figure 7.2. Given the observed values $A1, A2, \ldots, A4$ and a guess of the pass-key value, the corresponding $SRES'$ value can then be calculated. If the calculated value equals the observed value $SRES$, the attackers can check whether they have made a correct guess or not. If the size of the pass-key is smaller than the size of the $SRES$ value, they can be almost sure of whether or not the guess was correct. Furthermore, if the size of the pass-key value is small, they can check all possible values and see where they get a match between $SRES'$ and $SRES$. If further confidence is needed, the second authentication exchange can be used (mutual authentication is always performed at the pairing). Hence, short pass-key values do not protect the users from a passive eavesdropper or man in the middle present at the pairing occasion.

The security problems with short pass-key values have been reported in several papers and official reports. The Bluetooth specification also recommends the use of longer pass-keys for sensitive applications [18]. Jakobsson and Wetzel [19] indicated that it would be possible to obtain the link key at the initialization through passive eavesdropping or a man-in-the-middle attack. In a recent

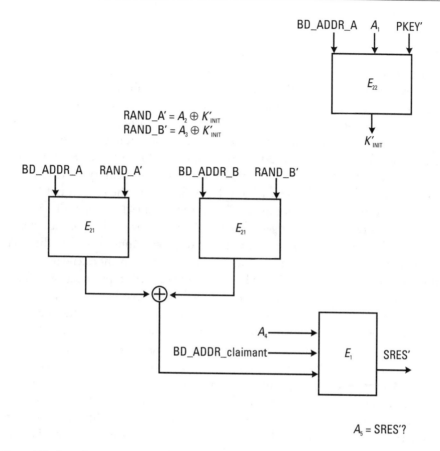

Figure 7.2 Pass-key test attack against the Bluetooth pairing.

National Institute of Standards and Technology (NIST) report [1], the problem with short pass-key values was listed as one of the main Bluetooth security vulnerabilities (together with unit key usage and privacy attacks). Vaino [20] also briefly discusses the short pass-key problem. In a more recent paper by Kügler [21], the passive eavesdropping attack on the pairing is described. To circumvent the attack, the author suggests the usage of long pass-keys. In Chapter 9 we describe alternative pairing methods that are not vulnerable to the attack we described in this section.

7.4 Improper key storage

In Section 3.7.3, different options for how to store the link key database are discussed. This section will discuss some possible consequences if the key database is not stored in a proper way.

7.4.1 Disclosure of keys

If a secret key is disclosed to an adversary, there is an obvious risk of an impersonation attack—simply use the stolen key and the *BD_ADDR* of the device from which the key was stolen. Therefore, the key database should not be readable to anyone in addition to the rightful owner. For small personal devices such as headsets and phones, the risk of losing keys to nonauthorized persons is rather small. To get such information out of these devices requires very good knowledge not only of where to find the information, but in many cases also special equipment to be able to read the device's nonvolatile memory. If that equipment is available, the adversary is most likely faced with the problem of finding the keys within a memory dump, as thin devices often lack a proper file system.

For more advanced gadgets that use Bluetooth, the risk of key disclosure increases. For instance, a network-connected desktop computer at the office may be equipped with a Bluetooth USB plug to facilitate convenient calendar synchronization to a mobile phone. If the key database is stored in plaintext on a file of that computer, there are many ways of getting hold of that file. In the worst case, it is possible to connect remotely (via the intranet) and simply read the content of the file. Alternatively, someone may sit down in front of the computer while the owner is having lunch and quickly copy the file to a diskette or mail it.

A variation on this theme involves a malicious USB plug or Personal Computer Memory Card International Association (PCMCIA) card (also known as PC-card). The rightful Bluetooth device attached to the computer may be exchanged for a false one, whose only purpose is to "suck" out link keys from the host. To accomplish this attack, a Link Key Request event is issued by the false device. Normally, this event indicates to the host that the link manager needs a link key for a particular device (the *BD_ADDR* is a parameter of this event) in order to perform authentication. However, in this scenario the false device simply does this to read the link key for a particular *BD_ADDR*. If there is a match in the database, the key will be returned in the HCI Link Key Request Reply command. In case there is no match in the database, the HCI Link Key Request Negative Reply will be sent. Clearly, the false Bluetooth device can repeat this for several addresses of interest. Upon completion, the adversary removes the false device containing valid link keys—its content may be used for impersonation attacks later on.

In case the link key database is stored in the module rather than on the host, a similar attack may take place. The rightful USB plug or PCMCIA card is removed from the owner's computer and inserted into a corresponding slot of the adversary's computer. On this computer, a program runs that issues the HCI Read Stored Link Key command to the attached Bluetooth device. This HCI command is used to read out one or more keys stored on the Bluetooth controller. The controller responds with a list of known link keys/address pairs in the `Return Link Keys` event. Once the list of keys has been read out, the USB plug (or card) is returned to its proper owner, who may be completely unaware that the device went missing for some time.

The two last examples illustrate the importance of protecting the interface between the Bluetooth host (computer) and the Bluetooth controller (module) whenever these are physically separated. Ideally, every removable Bluetooth device should be paired with the host(s) it is allowed to run on. Conversely, the host should only communicate with controllers to whom it has a trusted relationship.

Another advanced attack involves malicious software. A *Trojan horse* disguised as something quite innocent can send the key database to some place where the adversary can access it. If this malicious code is distributed through a virus or worm, the attack can quickly spread to a large number of computers. In fact, the adversary need not know a priori who has Bluetooth installed and is therefore a promising victim; if the virus infects a good percentage of the desktop computers at an enterprise site, chances are good that at least some candidates are found.

Once the link key of a computer and phone (and the *BD_ADDR* of the computer) is known, the adversary can "silently" connect to the mobile phone, impersonate the computer, and make use of any service the phone offers over Bluetooth (e.g., voice and data calls).

7.4.2 Tampering with keys

A possible way to gain unauthorized access to a Bluetooth-equipped device is by adding a link key to its key database without proper pairing. Then, when a connection attempt is being made, the link manager of the device under attack will assume that a valid bonding to the intruder exists, as there is a link key stored in its database. In case the link key is marked as belonging to a trusted device (see Section 6.1.1), the adversary will gain unconditional access to all Bluetooth services running on the host of the attacked device. In principle, the same conditions apply as were discussed in Section 7.4.1 for being able to deploy this attack. Thin devices are not very susceptible, as the practicalities of tampering with their key databases are quite complex. Regular computers are a more likely target. Again, having the key database writable for anyone in addition to the rightful owner is a bad thing. Encrypting the file will help, as it will be much harder to plant known link keys there, even if the adversary is capable of writing to or exchanging the key database file. One may also choose to integrity protect the key database.

7.4.3 Denial of service

An attacker has different options when it comes to destroying the content of the key database. If an attacker wipes out the file, removes one or more keys, or corrupts the content to make it into unintelligible garbage, the damage will be apparent when an authentication attempt is made. In Section 3.7.3, the way this is detected is discussed, depending on the current role as verifier or claimant. The specification does not mandate how to proceed when a corrupted database is detected. Clearly, one option is to alert the user, who can then initiate a new pairing to the devices that are affected.

A clever adversary who knows the format of the database may bypass detection by manipulating the key and a corresponding CRC (if present) such that this checks also for the corrupted key(s). This is analogous to what was discussed in Section 7.2. In this case, the error will not be detected until the authentication fails (i.e., the response *SRES* of the claimant does not match what the verifier calculated). At this point, the verifier aborts the link by sending the `LMP detach` PDU with the authentication failure error code. Furthermore, according to the specification, the LM of the verifier will not allow new authentication attempts from the claimant until a certain waiting interval has expired. For each failed authentication attempt, this waiting interval will grow exponentially. The purpose of this is to prevent an intruder from trying many keys in a short time. Unfortunately, in this case the effect is that a device that should have been granted access is locked out—for each failed attempt the user will see a longer waiting time without understanding what is going on. The only way to break this circle is to erase the old set of keys by requiring a new pairing.

One way to avoid the latter form of attack is to add some form of integrity protection to the key database. This comes in the form of extra parity bits that are computed as a nonlinear function, that is, a *message authentication code* of the stored information in the database and a secret key. An adversary has a very low probability of succeeding in changing any part of the information such that it will not be detected by the user, as long as the number of parity bits are large enough and the secret key is not disclosed. Clearly, it is important to protect the key sufficiently. In some systems, it may be feasible to hide the key in nonvolatile memory that is not accessible from any visible bus, such as on-chip ROM that cannot be read from external pins on the chip set.

7.5   Unit key

The authentication and encryption mechanisms based on unit keys are the same as those based on combination keys. However, a unit that uses a unit key is only able to use one key for all its secure connections. Hence, it has to share this key with all other units that it trusts. Consequently, a trusted device (a device that possesses the unit key) that eavesdrops on the initial authentication messages between two other units that utilize the unit key will be able to eavesdrop on any traffic between these two units. A trusted unit that has modified its own device address is also able to impersonate the unit distributing the unit key. Thus, when using a unit key, there is no protection against attacks from trusted devices. The unit key usage weakness was observed by Jakobsson and Wetzel in [19] and was also pointed out by NIST in a report on wireless security [22]. The potential risks with units keys have also been recognized by the Bluetooth SIG. Originally, the unit key was introduced in order to reduce memory requirements on very limited devices and remains part of the standard for backward compatibility reasons. The Bluetooth combination keys would be much more appropriate to use for almost any Bluetooth unit and the Bluetooth SIG does not recommend the use of unit keys [23] anymore.

7.6 Location tracking

As we have discussed, security in computer networks includes different aspects of message integrity, authentication, and confidentiality. In wireless networks, where users move between different networks and media types, another issue becomes important: *location privacy*. Since the Bluetooth technology is targeted toward devices of personal type like mobile phones, PDAs, or laptops, this becomes a real issue. The location privacy threat is actually independent of whether Bluetooth is just used for local connectivity or as an access technology. As long as the device is carried and used by one particular person, there is a risk that the device is tracked using the transmitted radio signals from the Bluetooth-enabled device. In order to be able to track user movements, there must be some fixed device identity the attacker can utilize. Once the attacker has succeeded in linking a human identity to the device identity, the threat becomes a reality. Hence, all kinds of fixed identities are potential privacy threats. The Bluetooth device address or any value derived from the device address is the obvious location privacy attack target in Bluetooth. Moreover, even a user-friendly name or any other application-specific identity might be a privacy problem. In this section we discuss the Bluetooth device address usage from a privacy perspective and discuss different Bluetooth location tracking attacks.

To protect a device against location tracking, an anonymity mode is needed. Devices operating in anonymous mode regularly update their device address by randomly choosing a new one. The anonymity mode is described in detail in Chapter 8.

7.6.1 Bluetooth device address and location tracking

The most serious location tracking threat utilizes the Bluetooth device address. The address format is derived from the IEEE 802 standard. The Bluetooth device address, BD_ADDR, has a length of 48 bits and consists of three different parts:

1. Lower address part;

2. Upper address part (UAP);

3. Nonsignificant address part (NAP).

The format is illustrated in Figure 7.3. The LAP and UAP form the significant part.

The entire Bluetooth address (LAP, UAP, and NAP parts) is sent in the special *frequency hop synchronization* (FHS) packets transmitted at certain occasions. This fact can be utilized in the different attacks described in Section 7.6.2. However, this is not the only threat. Any deterministic value derived from the entire or parts of a fixed device address might be used for the very same purpose. This is the case for the Bluetooth access codes. These codes form the first part of each packet transmitted in Bluetooth. There are three different distinct access codes:

1. CAC, which is derived from the master's LAP;

2. *Device access code* (DAC), which is derived form the specific device's (slave) LAP;

3. *Inquiry access code* (IAC), which can be of two different forms, but is derived from special dedicated LAP values not related to any specific *BD_ADDR.*

Hence, the CAC and DAC (but not the IAC) can potentially be used to track the location of a specific user.

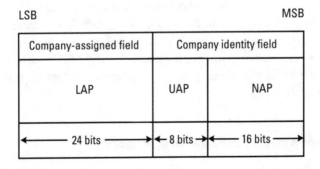

Figure 7.3 Bluetooth device address format.

7.6.2 Five different types of location tracking attacks

As we just discussed, directly or indirectly, the use of a fixed device address allows the general location of Bluetooth devices to be clandestinely determined. The device address, the CAC, or the DAC can be used to identify a particular device. Also, the user-friendly name of a device can be used to track the location of a device. In all, five different types of location tracking attacks have been identified. We describe these in the following sections.

Inquiry attack

In this scenario the attacker has distributed one or more Bluetooth devices throughout a region in which he desires to locate Bluetooth users. This can be done relatively inexpensively due to the low cost of Bluetooth devices. In addition, this network of devices can be used for a legitimate purpose, such as public information kiosks, and thus may already exist. Furthermore, assume that the potential victim of such an attack has left his device in discoverable mode. In this case, the attacking device can simply interrogate the area using frequent inquiry messages for devices and maintain a log of all the device addresses that are discovered. This data can be correlated with time to provide an accurate record of victim movements and associations (e.g., two people who are frequently in the same area are probably associated in some way).

Traffic monitoring attack

The next attack we describe succeeds even if the victim device is not in discoverable mode. In this case, the attacker simply monitors the communication between two trusted devices belonging to the victim. These devices will communicate using a specific CAC. This CAC is computed from the device address of the master device in the piconet. Therefore, an attacker can determine the master devices in the area by simply monitoring all network traffic nearby. Even if the CAC is not unique, the attacker can be quite confident that a particular CAC belongs to one unique device due to the small probability of two devices that have the same CAC within a small area. Similarly, the DAC can be used to detect a particular device. Furthermore, the whole device address is sent in the FHS packets of the devices, allowing an attacker to uniquely determine the identity of a device. An attack based on monitoring DAC or FHS packets are not as powerful as an attack based on monitoring CAC, since the FHS packet or packets containing DAC are only used at connection establishment (or at the master-slave switch), that is, events that are relatively rare.

Paging attack

This attack allows the attacker to determine if a given device with a known *BD_ADDR* or DAC is present within range. The attack requires that the victim's device is connectable. The attacking device pages the target device, waits for the ID packet to be returned, and then does not respond. If an ID is returned, then the attacker knows that the victim device is present. The target device, waiting for the response, will just time out and the incident will not be reported to the application layer.

Frequency hopping attack

The frequency hopping scheme in Bluetooth is determined by a repeating hopping sequence. The hopping scheme is calculated from different input parameters, such as an address and the master clock. In the connection state, the LAP and the four least significant bits in the UAP of the master device are used. In the page state, the LAP/UAP of the paged unit is used. Thus, it is (at least theoretically) possible to get information of the LAP and four bits in the UAP based on the observed hopping scheme.

User-friendly name attack

The Bluetooth LMP command, `LMP name req`, can be used to request the user-friendly name anytime after a successful baseband paging procedure. The name request LMP command can be used to mount a location tracking attack. Such an attack is based on simply requesting the device user-friendly name. The attack will succeed if the victim device is connectable and has a unique user-friendly name defined.

7.7 Implementation flaws

No matter how good the security functionality a technology specifies, a bad or broken implementation can jeopardize all of it. Of course, Bluetooth is no exception to this rule. The technology is relatively young and quite complex. In general, it is very difficult to test a product in every conceivable setting it may end up being used in. The manufacturers tend to focus their efforts on interoperability issues, which is understandable, as behavioral compliance tests are mandated in the product qualification process. Unfortunately, only the basic security functionality can be verified in the qualification process, such as pairing, authentication, and setting up an encrypted link. Many other aspects that are not mandated in the specification are not tested but do have an impact on the overall security. These aspects include (but are not limited to): security policy enforcement, key database management, user interaction, and memory read/write protection. Clearly, there is a risk that something that seemed to work in the laboratory is released as a product with a security-related flaw in its implementation.

Recently there have been claims of Bluetooth vulnerabilities [24] that can be attributed to broken implementations. The claims have to some extent been confirmed by some mobile phone manufacturers. Three types of attacks with the following properties are mentioned.

Snarf attack. The attacker is able to set up a connection to an (unpaired) victim's device without alerting the victim or requiring the victim's consent. After doing this, the attacker is able to access restricted portions of the victim's personal data, such as the phone book, address book, and calendar.

Backdoor attack. First, the attacker needs to establish a trust relation with the victim's Bluetooth device. Then, the attacker "erases" the entry of the established link from the victim's list of paired devices without erasing it from the victim's link key database. After this is accomplished, the attacker is able to access the services and data of the target device as before, but without the owner's knowledge or consent.

Bluejacking. This is a term used for sending unsolicited messages to other Bluetooth devices [25]. It can be accomplished by sending a business card or phone book entry in which the name field has been filled in with a message rather than a real name. Upon reception, the name field is usually displayed together with an appended question of whether the message should be saved to the contact list or not. Clearly, while this could be annoying, it is not a real threat to security. It is simply another name for the *object push* of the OBEX protocol, which is implemented in most Bluetooth-enabled phones, laptops, and PDAs.

While the authenticity of the snarf and backdoor attacks are not fully confirmed, they do show the importance of implementing and enforcing the security policies correctly. For instance, manufacturers of Bluetooth products must ensure that a remote device is not mistakenly granted access to all services on the local device just because a particular service is opened for it. One way to handle this is by implementing a security manager along the lines discussed in Chapter 6.

References

[1]   NIST, "Wireless Network Security 801.11, Bluetooth and Hand Held Devices," Technical Report Special Publications 800-48, U.S. Department of Commerce/NIST, National Technical Information Service, Springfield, VA, April 2002.

[2]   Anderson, R., "Searching for the Optimum Correlation Attack," in B. Preneel, (ed.), *Fast Software Encryption FSE'94*, No. 1008 in LNCS, 1995, pp. 137–143.

[3]   Meier, W., and O. Staffelbach, "Fast Correlation Attacks on Certain Stream Ciphers," *J. Cryptology*, Vol. 1, 1989, pp. 159–176. (Appeared also in *Proc. Eurocrypt 88*, No. 330 LNCS, 1988).

[4]   Meier, W., and O. Staffelbach, "Correlation Properties of Combiners with Memory in Stream Ciphers," *J. Cryptology*, Vol. 5, No. 1, 1992, pp. 67–86.

[5]   Hermelin, M., and K. Nyberg, "Correlation Properties of the Bluetooth Summation Combiner," in J. Song, ed., *Proc. ICISC'99, 1999 International Conf. Information Security and Cryptography*, No. 1787 in LNCS, Berlin: Springer-Verlag, December 2000, pp. 17–29.

[6]   Massey, J. L., and R. A. Rueppel, "Method of, and Apparatus for, Transforming a Digital Sequence into an Encoded Form," U.S. Patent No. 4,797,922, 1989.

[7]   Fluhrer, S., and S. Lucks, "Analysis of the E_0 Cryptosystem," in A. M. Youssef S. Vaudenay, ed., *Proc. Selected Areas in Cryptography 01*, No. 2259 in LNCS, Berlin: Springer-Verlag, 2001, pp. 38–48.

[8]   Krause, M., "Bdd Based Cryptanalysis of Keystream Generators," *Proc. Eurocrypt 02*, No. 2332 in LNCS, Berlin: Springer-Verlag, 2002, pp. 222–237.

[9]   Bagini, V., J. Golic, and G. Morgari, "Linear Cryptanalysis of Bluetooth Stream Cipher," in L. R. Knudsen, (ed.), *Proc. Eurocrypt 02*, No. 2332 in LNCS, Berlin: Springer-Verlag, 2002, pp. 238–255.

[10] Ekdahl, P., and T. Johansson, "Some Results on Correlations in the Bluetooth Stream Cipher," *Proc. 10th Joint Conf. Communication and Coding*, Austria, 2000, p. 16.

[11] Ekdahl, P., "On LFSR Based Stream Ciphers," Ph.D. thesis, Lund University, November 2003.

[12] Armknecht, F., A Linearization Attack on the Bluetooth Key Stream Generator, available at http://eprint.iacr.org/2002/191, accessed November 2002.

[13] Armknecht, F., and M. Krause, "Algebraic Attacks on Combiners with Memory," *Proc. Crypto 03*, No. 2729 in LNCS, Berlin: Springer-Verlag, 2003, pp. 162–176.

[14] Courtois, N., "Fast Algebraic Attacks on Stream Ciphers with Linear Feedback," *Proc. Crypto 03*, No. 2729 in LNCS, Berlin: Springer-Verlag, 2003, pp. 176–194.

[15] Courtois, N., et al., "Efficient Algorithms for Solving Overdefined Systems of Multivariate Polynomial Equations," *Proc. Eurocrypt 00*, No. 1807 in LNCS, Berlin: Springer-Verlag, 2000, pp. 392–407.

[16] Coppersmith, D., and S. Winograd, "Matrix Multiplication via Arithmetic Progressions," *J. Symbolic Computation*, Vol. 9, 1990, pp. 251–280.

[17] Courtois, N., "Higher Order Correlation Attacks, XL Algorithm and Crypt Analysis of Toyocrypt," in P. J. Lee and C. H. Lim, (eds.), *Proc. Information Security and Cryptology*, ICISC 2002, No. 2587 in LNCS, Berlin: Springer-Verlag, 2003, pp. 182–199.

[18] Bluetooth Special Interest Group, *Specification of the Bluetooth System, Version 1.2, Core System Package*, November 2003.

[19]   Jakobsson, M., and S. Wetzel, "Security Weaknesses in Bluetooth," in D. Naccache, ed., *Proc. RSA Conf. 2001*, No. 2020 in LNCS, Berlin: Springer-Verlag.

[20]   Vainio, J., "Bluetooth Security," available at http://www.niksula.cs.hut.fi/~jiitv/bluesec.html, accessed May 2000.

[21]   Kügler, D., "Man in the Middle Attacks on Bluetooth, Revised Papers," in R. N. Wright, (ed.), *Financial Cryptography, 7th International Con., FC 2003*, No. 2742 in LNCS, Berlin: Springer-Verlag, 2003, pp. 149–61.

[22]   Karygiannis, T., and L. Owens, "Wireless Network Security, 802.11, Bluetooth and Handheld Devices," *NIST Special Publication 800-48*, November 2002.

[23]   Gehrmann, C., ed., "Bluetooth Security White Paper," White Paper Revision 1.0, Bluetooth SIG, April 2002.

[24]   Laurie, A., and B. Laurie, "Serious Flaws in Bluetooth Security Lead to Disclosure of Personal Data," available at http://www.bluestumbler.org/, accessed November 2003.

[25]   bluejackQ with a Q, available at http://www.bluejackQ.com/whatis.htm, accessed November 2003.

Part II:
Bluetooth Security Enhancements

8

Providing Anonymity

In Chapter 7 we described different types of location tracking attacks against Bluetooth units. These threats show that some important security features are lacking in the Bluetooth standard. This has motivated the development of a new Bluetooth mode of operation that provides protection against the location privacy threat. We call the new mode a Bluetooth *anonymity mode*. This mode of operation is currently not part of the Bluetooth standard. Special care has been taken to make this mode of operation have good interoperability with devices not supporting the anonymity mode. The anonymity might be included in a future release of the Bluetooth specification.

As previously explained, location tracking can be based on the *BD_ADDR*, channel access code, or the device access code. The best way to protect against location tracking would be to regularly change the device address. This is also the basic idea in the anonymity mode. However, normal Bluetooth functionality must also be provided if the device address is changed. In this chapter we describe how this can be dealt with.

8.1   Overview of the anonymity mode

The regular address changes necessary for anonymity result in new address management and new addresses being introduced. Three address types are suggested: *fixed address, active address,* and *alias address.* The active address is randomly selected, and anonymous devices base the Bluetooth access codes on this address. Recall that the access code can be used to track the location of a device. Rules for how and when the active address is updated are given. It is actually also the case that the different address behavior for anonymous devices implies that inquiry and paging must be handled a little bit differently than for nonanonymous devices. This is primarily handled by using three different connectable modes: *connectable mode, private connectable mode,* and *general connectable mode.* The secure identification in anonymity mode is built on the usage of the alias addresses and the so-called *alias authentication.* Also, the pairing has to be slightly changed in order to allow anonymous devices to securely page and identify each other. All these new features mean that some additional control signaling is needed and that some new LMP commands need to be defined.

8.2 Address usage

In this section, the addresses and address usage for devices supporting the anonymous mode are described. In contrast to ordinary Bluetooth, fixed addresses cannot be used for all purposes. Therefore, new addresses are introduced and the device address is used in a little bit different way than in the Bluetooth 1.2 specification. This also means that a slightly new and different terminology is used. The anonymity mode makes use of three different kinds of device addresses:

1. Fixed device address, *BD_ADDR_fixed;*
2. Active device address, *BD_ADDR;*
3. Alias addresses, *BD_ADDR_alias.*

In the following sections, the different addresses and how they are used in the anonymity mode are discussed.

8.2.1 The fixed device address, *BD_ADDR_fixed*

Each Bluetooth transceiver is allocated a unique 48-bit Bluetooth device address (*BD_ADDR_fixed*)[1] from the manufacturer. The *BD_ADDR_fixed* consists of three parts: LAP, UAP, and NAP. Figure 7.3 in Chapter 7 shows the address field sizes and the format. The fixed address is derived from the IEEE 802 standard [1]. The LAP and UAP form the significant part of the *BD_ADDR.*

The fixed address is used to allow a device to directly page another device that it has previously been paired with. Without a fixed address that can be used for this purpose, the devices would always need to repeat the inquiry procedure. Obviously, this would result in very slow connection setup. However, in order not to jeopardize the anonymity, these addresses shall only be used between trusted devices (see Section 8.6).

---

1. This address corresponds to the ordinary Bluetooth device address.

8.2.2 The active device address, *BD_ADDR*

The *BD_ADDR* is the active device address, and anonymous devices regularly update this address (more detail is given below). Devices not supporting the anonymity mode or devices in nonanonymous mode only use one address, *BD_ADDR*. Actually, for such devices the *BD_ADDR* always equals the *BD_ADDR_fixed* (see previous section).

Anonymous devices use the active address as a replacement for an ordinary fixed address for connection establishment and communication. Since the address is changed all the time, it will not be possible to track a device based on this address.

The *BD_ADDR* has exactly the same format as *BD_ADDR_fixed* and consists of three parts: LAP, UAP, and NAP. The UAP and NAP parts are fixed and shall be chosen to a nondevice-specific value. In particular, they can be chosen to a value that does not overlap with any company assigned IEEE MAC address space [1]. This is accomplished, for example, by using the locally assigned IEEE MAC address space [1]. The LAP part of the *BD_ADDR* needs to be chosen uniformly and at random. It can take any value except the 64 reserved LAP values for general and dedicated inquiry, that is, values from `0x9E8B00` to `0x9E8B33`.

In order to combat the location tracking threat, anonymous devices regularly update the active LAP. The rules for when the address shall be updated are given below. A LAP value is generated by selecting uniformly at random any value between `0x000000` and `0xFFFFFF`. If the value falls within the reserved LAP range, that is, values from `0x9E8B00` to `0x9E8B33`, a new random LAP value is generated. This procedure is repeated until a value outside the range is obtained.

The LAP updating is determined by two time parameters. The parameters are:

1. Update period, $T_{\text{ADDR update}}$;
2. Time period reserved for inquiry, $T_{\text{ADDR inquiry period}}$.

The update period tells how often the device shall attempt to update the active address. The parameter $T_{\text{ADDR inquiry period}}$ tells how long a time a device must wait before it is allowed to update the active address after it has sent the current address in an inquiry response message.

The basic principle is that a device shall update the address every $T_{\text{ADDR update}}$ seconds. However, if this updating occasion happens to be when the device has just sent the current address in an inquiry response, any unit trying to connect to the anonymous device would fail with the connection request. For this reason the updating waiting period defined by the second parameter $T_{\text{ADDR inquiry period}}$ has been introduced. In addition, there shall be no update if the device is acting as a master device and has connections with devices not supporting the anonymous node. Otherwise, the CAC will change and the legacy devices would immediately lose the connection when the CAC is changed. These facts provide the motivation for the updating rules used for updating the active address.

The detailed updating rules are shown in the flow diagram in Figure 8.1. The updating flow is as follows:

1. A new LAP is always generated at power-up.

2. Two time variables are set, $t_1 = 0$ and $t_2 = T_{\text{ADDR inquiry period}} + 1$. t_1 measures the general updating intervals and t_2 measures the time from the last use of the "old address" in an inquiry response. (At the start, t_2 is set to a value greater than the defined updating waiting period after inquiry response, $T_{\text{ADDR inquiry period}}$.)

3. The *BD_ADDR* is updated and the first timer t_1 is started.

4. A loop is created where the timer t_1 is continuously checked. If the timer exceeds the updating period, $T_{\text{ADDR update}}$, the looping process stops. If an inquiry response message is returned during the execution of the loop, the second timer t_2 is set to zero and started.

5. If t_2 is less than or equal to $T_{\text{ADDR inquiry period}}$, return to the loop in step 4.

6. If the device has no existing connections, a new LAP is generated, followed by a jump to step 2.

7. A new loop is entered. The loop runs as long as the device has any connection with a device not supporting the anonymity mode or any parked device, or if the device is parked itself. If there are no connections when the loops ends, a new LAP is generated, followed by a jump back to step 2.

8. A new LAP is generated. If the device is not a master in any piconet, the new (not yet updated) *BD_ADDR* is sent to all connected devices using the new LMP command, **LMP active address** (see Section 8.7). Then jump to step 2.

9. The switch instant time, T_s is chosen. It should be chosen such that the master will be able to inform all connected slaves of the new *BD_ADDR* before the instant is reached. Next the master sends the new *BD_ADDR* (not yet updated) and the switch instant T_s to all slaves using the new LMP command **LMP active address** (see Section 8.7). When the instant is reached, jump back to step 2.

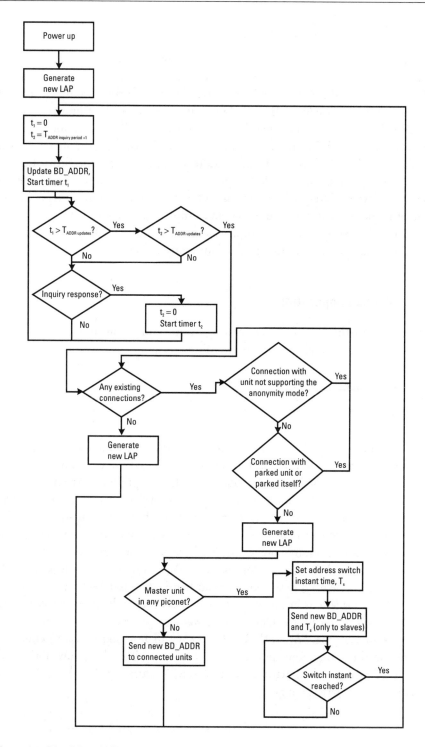

Figure 8.1 The *BD_ADDR* updating rules.

8.2.3   Alias addresses, *BD_ADDR_alias*

Since it is not possible to identify other anonymous devices based on their *BD_ADDR* when they are operating in the anonymous mode, anonymous devices must make use of an alternative device identifier in the Bluetooth authentication procedure. Also, the authentication procedure must be slightly modified. The new procedure, alias authentication, will be described in more detail in Section 8.5. The alias authentication is based on the usage of *alias addresses*, *BD_ADDR_alias*. An alias address is used purely for authentication purposes. For simplicity, the *BD_ADDR_alias* can be chosen to 48 bits like any ordinary device address. All the bits should be chosen uniformly, independently, and at random. Hence, the address field cannot be divided into any meaningful subfields. The support and use of alias addresses and authentication are necessary for making authentication in the anonymity mode work.

8.3   Modes of operation

In order to distinguish devices operating in the anonymous mode from devices that are not anonymous, we define two different modes of operation:

1. Nonanonymous;

2. Anonymous.

A Bluetooth device can only operate in one of these modes at a time. Both modes are in principle fully backward compatible with devices not supporting these new modes. The latter, of course, with the exception that the new features introduced in the anonymous mode cannot be utilized with standard devices. One can say that for anonymous devices, Bluetooth devices not supporting the anonymous mode will look like devices that always operate in nonanonymous mode. Devices in anonymous mode shall regularly update the active device address, *BD_ADDR* (see Section 8.2). In addition, devices supporting the anonymous mode need to support alias authentication (see Section 8.5).

When a device is in nonanonymous mode, it uses the fixed device address in all its communications. Devices that want to prevent the location tracking attacks based on the *BD_ADDR*, CAC, DAC, or hopping sequence choose to operate in the anonymous mode. Location tracking is in the anonymous mode prevented by regularly updating the active device address, as it is the address that is visible on the wireless link.

8.4 Inquiry and paging

With respect to inquiry, there is no difference between anonymous and nonanonymous devices. A device can be either in discoverable or nondiscoverable mode. Devices in discoverable mode return their active device address (see Section 8.2) in the inquiry response message. This implies that anonymous devices return a random address, while nonanonymous devices return the fixed device address.

With respect to paging, a Bluetooth device can be either in nonconnectable mode or in connectable mode. We have slightly changed the latter mode of operation for anonymous units and split it into three new modes:

1. Connectable mode;
2. Private connectable mode;
3. General connectable mode.

We discuss the rationale behind these three modes in more detail below. Devices in nonconnectable mode never perform any page scans. Hence, it is not possible to initiate any connections with a nonconnectable device.

The page procedure consists of a number of steps. The procedure starts with the device trying to find the address of the device it wants to connect to. A device in anonymous mode can be paged based on two possible addresses, the active device address and the fixed device address. Since an anonymous device in discoverable mode returns the active address in the inquiry response message, the paging device can use the inquiry procedure to find the active address of discoverable devices nearby. If the devices have performed a *private pairing* (see Section 8.6), the paging device knows the fixed address of the other device. In this case, paging using the fixed device address of the other device is possible. The address of the paged device is used to determine the page hopping sequence. A device can choose whether it shall be reachable on the active address, the fixed address, or both the fixed and active addresses. This corresponds to the different connectable modes that we have defined for the anonymity mode.

8.4.1 Connectable mode

When a standard Bluetooth device is in connectable mode, it periodically enters the page scan state. The device makes page scans using the ordinary fixed device address. Anonymous devices operating in connectable mode use the same principles but make page scans on the active device address, *BD_ADDR*. The device can use different types of page scanning schemes. The connection setup time depends on the scanning interval and is a trade-off between power consumption, available bandwidth, and setup delay. Scan interval, scan window, and interlaced scan can be used to achieve the desired trade-off (see [2] for details). Three different page scan modes are defined in the Bluetooth specification, and they are called R0, R1, and R2, respectively. In R0, continuous scanning is used, while R1 uses a scan interval of at the most 1.28 sec and R2 a maximum of 2.56 sec. A device in connectable mode can use any of the available scan modes.

The connectable mode was introduced to allow any device to connect to an anonymous device. Typically, the active address is obtained through the inquiry procedure. Once the active address is known and the anonymous device is in connectable mode, it will be possible to connect to the device using a page on the active address.

8.4.2   Private connectable mode

The private connectable mode needs to be introduced to allow a device to directly page another device. By direct we mean that the device does not need to first go through the inquiry procedure. The inquiry procedure can take a rather long time. Furthermore, a device would like to connect to another device without being forced to answer responses from unknown devices. Hence, when a Bluetooth device is in private connectable mode, it makes page scans using the Bluetooth fixed device address, *BD_ADDR_fixed*. Any of the three different page scanning modes, R0, R1, or R2 (see Section 8.4.1), can be used.

The private connectable mode allows direct establishment of connections between trusted devices. Ideally a device only shares the value of the fixed address with trusted devices. This means that this connection mode should only be used by a device when it expects connection requests from trusted devices. Thus, even if the fixed address is not a secret parameter in a strict sense, a device that cares about location privacy should be careful about spreading the fixed address. If the fixed address is compromised, there is a small risk that the device could be tracked using the paging attack described in Chapter 7. This threat can be avoided by never entering the nonanonymous or private connectable mode. On the other hand, that makes it impossible to set up direct connections between trusted devices.

Hence, to reduce this threat, a device shall always expect an alias authentication request (see Section 8.5) from the master after a response to a paging on the fixed address. If no alias is received or the setup fails before the connection state has been reached, we recommend a connection failure counter to be incremented. If the failure counter exceeds a threshold value, the host controller can then send a warning to the host. It is then up to the host to take proper action and perhaps warn the user that someone might try to track the movement using the paging attack.

8.4.3 General connectable mode

When a Bluetooth device is in general connectable mode, it makes page scans on both the Bluetooth active device address, *BD_ADDR*, and the fixed device address, *BD_ADDR-fixed*. This makes it possible for a device to accept Bluetooth connections from both trusted known devices and unknown devices (through the inquiry procedure). A device in general connectable mode makes two consecutive page scans at each scanning occasion. Only the scanning modes R1 or R2 can be used in general connectable mode and not R0. The first scan is based on the page hopping sequence derived from the *BD_ADDR* and the second scan is based on the page hopping sequence derived from the *BD_ADDR-fixed*. Since R0 is not supported, fast connection setup cannot be achieved by using continuous scanning. When very fast connection setups are required, it is possible to use two consecutive R1 page scans with interlaced scan and very short page scan interval. The paging attack (see Section 7.6.2) applies also to the general connectable mode. To reduce the risk for this attack, a device shall always expect an alias authentication request (see Section 8.5) from the master after making a response to a paging on the fixed address. If no alias is received or the setup fails before the connection state has been reached, a connection failure counter can be incremented (see Section 8.4.2).

8.5 Alias authentication

As we have discussed, anonymous devices regularly update the active device address. Hence, the active address cannot be used to identify devices. This is not strange, since the whole idea with the anonymity mode is that it should not be possible to identify devices. However, this causes problems when trusted devices would like to authenticate each other and set up secure connections without repeated pairing. We introduce alias authentication to solve this problem. Alias authentication is a method to disconnect the link key dependency on the (physical) device address and an alias address is used as a link key identifier. To be more precise, alias authentication allows authentication based on an alias address instead of the active or fixed device address. By exchanging alias addresses after a link is established but before authentication takes place, the involved devices are able to find the link key associated with the established link. This possibility is useful not only for anonymous devices but for other purposes as well. One example is when a device attaches to a network access point and the device wishes to authenticate to the network rather than the access point (see Section 10.2).

Alias addresses are used to identify a security association between a pair of devices (or a network and a device). Denote two devices in a pair by *A* and *B*. In the symmetric case, two alias addresses are used. One address, $BD\_ADDR\_alias_A$, is used by device B to identify device A, and the other address, $BD\_ADDR\_alias_B$, is used by device A to identify device B. Alias authentication can also be used in an asymmetric fashion. In that case, only one of the devices in the pair uses an alias address to authenticate the other device. The other device in the pair is identified (for mutual authentication) using the fixed address. If both devices are operating in anonymous mode, symmetric alias authentication will apply and the devices exchange two alias addresses, one for each device.

For the anonymity mode, we propose a special pairing procedure. During this pairing procedure, the devices exchange alias and fixed addresses (see Section 8.6). A device supporting alias authentication needs to maintain an alias database (part of the key and device database). The alias database maps alias addresses to link keys. Device A stores $BD\_ADDR\_alias_A$ together with the link key, the alias address used to identify device B ($BD\_ADDR\_alias_B$), and the fixed address of device B ($BD\_ADDR\text{-}fixed_B$) in its database. (The fixed address is sent to the device over an encrypted link at the pairing occasion. See Section 8.6.) Similarly, device B stores $BD\_ADDR\_alias_B$ together with the link key, the alias address used to identify device A ($BD\_ADDR\_alias_A$), and the fixed address of device A ($BD\_ADDR\text{-}fixed_A$) in its database.

We propose to use the same format as the BD_ADDR for the alias addresses. The 48 bits shall be chosen uniformly at random by devices A and B (see also Section 8.2.3). The alias addresses should be updated at each new connection between A and B. If this is not the case, there is a risk that the device is instead tracked based on the alias address. It is most convenient if the new alias is generated by the "owner" of the alias address; that is, device A updates $BD\_ADDR\_alias_A$ and device B updates $BD\_ADDR\_alias_B$. The updated address is only allowed to be sent over an encrypted channel.

In the case of an application that uses the same alias for several different devices (e.g., see Section 10.2), the updated address might be the same as the previous. However, this principle shall only be used when alias addresses are not used for anonymity purposes.

At the next connection setup, the $BD\_ADDR\_alias_A$ and $BD\_ADDR\_alias_B$ need to be sent before authentication (but after a check that the corresponding device supports alias authentication) is performed. If this is not done, it is impossible for the devices to identify the right link key to use. Device A should send its $BD\_ADDR\_alias_A$ and device B should respond with $BD\_ADDR\_alias_B$ (see also the example in Section 8.8). The alias addresses are then used by the devices to find the correct link key. The link key is then used to perform mutual authentication and calculate the encryption key that is needed for the connection to be encrypted.

8.6 Pairing

For anonymous devices, we would like the user to decide (at the pairing) whether to disclose the fixed hardware address or not. Higher location privacy is achieved if the fixed address is only disclosed to trusted devices. By this we mean devices that can be trusted for a long time. This is not true for all pairings, as trust relations might as well be quite temporary. Thus, at the pairing, anonymous devices need to distinguish between devices to which the fixed address should be given and other devices. This is done by setting the device to *pairable* or *private pairable* mode. In the first pairing mode, the fixed address is not disclosed, while it is in the second. This is different from standard Bluetooth units that only support two pairing modes: *nonpairable* and *pairable*.

When a device supporting the anonymity mode is in pairable mode, it accepts a request for pairing through the LMP command LMP in rand from a remote device. It also issues this command if authentication is requested and no link key for the corresponding device is known. The device does not exchange alias addresses or private addresses with the remote device. The device shall reject all fixed address exchange requests, since it will not give out its own fixed address.

When a device is in private pairable mode, it also accepts requests for pairing and initiates a pairing if authentication is requested and the link key is missing. The device uses the new LMP commands (see Section 8.7) to exchange alias and private addresses.

The behavior of a device supporting the new private pairing modes needs to be carefully specified in order to provide good interoperability. We do not give any details here, but in the next section we list a set of LMP commands that can be used by the devices to exchange private addresses and alias addresses and in Section 8.8 we give a private pairing example.

8.7 Anonymity mode LMP commands

A set of new LMP commands are needed in order to inform connected devices of an update of the active address and to exchange alias and private addresses. In all, we have identified the need for three different anonymity mode LMP commands:

- LMP active address;

- LMP alias address;

- LMP fixed address.

In the following sections we describe how these command work in more detail.

8.7.1 Address update, `LMP active address`

Devices in anonymity mode maintain an active address that is changed frequently (see Section 8.2). The active address is used by the master to determine the hopping sequence and CAC used by the piconet. Hence, it is important for the master to inform the slaves of the new address whenever it is updated. Furthermore, a slave must also inform the master of updates to the active address. If this is not done, the master cannot directly reconnect (through paging) to the slave if the connection for some reason is broken or if a master-slave switch is required. The LMP command `LMP active address` can be used to inform other devices of active address updates as we now will describe.

When the master device decides to make a change to its active address, it informs all its slaves of the change. (See Section 8.2, where the updating rules are described in detail.) When a new LAP has been generated, the master should select a time instant that is far enough in the future that all slaves will have received the message and returned the `LMP accepted`. The master then needs to send the `LMP active address` PDU containing the new active address and the switching time to all slaves. When a slave receives the `LMP active address` PDU from the master, it shall return `LMP accepted` and start a timer to expire at the given time instant. The LMP PDU exchange sequence for a successful address exchange sequence is shown in Figure 8.2. When the switch instant is reached, the master shall change the active address, causing the hopping sequence, encryption, and CAC to change to values derived from the master's new active address.

Similarly, when a slave device decides to change its active address, it shall generate a new active address and send it to the master in the `LMP active address` PDU, as shown in Figure 8.2. No timing information is needed in this case, and the change in active address can take place immediately.

8.7.2 Alias address exchange, `LMP alias address`

As we described in Section 8.5, a device in anonymous mode needs to be authenticated based on a previously agreed-upon alias rather than on the

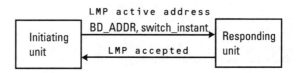

Figure 8.2 LMP sequence when informing a slave or master of a new active address.

BD_ADDR. The PDU `LMP alias address` can be used for this purpose. The PDU contains the alias address.

When a connection is being set up, either device may attempt to carry out the authentication using an alias. The initiating LM sends an `LMP alias address` PDU, which indicates an attempt to do authentication based on an alias. If the receiving LM knows of the specified alias, it replies with its own corresponding alias; otherwise it replies with `LMP not accepted`. The LMP PDU exchange sequence for a successful alias address exchange sequence is shown in Figure 8.3.

Once an alias has been established, subsequent authentications use the link key associated with the alias. When the connection is completed and encryption has been enabled, the master updates the alias address by generating a new alias address and sending it to the slave in an `LMP alias address`, which indicates a refresh of the *BD_ADDR_alias.* A special flag in the PDU is needed in order for the slave to be able to distinguish the alias address update case from the alias authentication case. The slave then replies with an update of its own corresponding alias according to the LM PDU exchange sequence in Figure 8.3. It is important that the alias address establishment or update messages are only sent on encrypted links; otherwise the anonymity might be compromised.

8.7.3 Fixed address exchange, `LMP fixed address`

As we described in Section 8.6, if one device is in the private pairing mode, the device sends its *BD_ADDR-fixed.* This is done in order to allow the other device to directly page (i.e., without going through the inquiry procedure) the device when a connection shall be established. The PDU `LMP fixed address` is used for this purpose. When a device receives this PDU and it is prepared to allow private pairing, it replies with its own fixed address as shown in the LM exchange sequence in Figure 8.4 (successful exchange sequence).

Figure 8.3 LMP sequence for successful exchange of alias addresses.

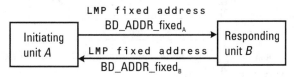

Figure 8.4 LMP sequence for successful exchange of fixed addresses.

The exchange of fixed addresses is only allowed to occur once encryption has been enabled for the connection to ensure that the anonymity is not compromised. Still, there is an anonymity risk with allowing usage of fixed addresses at all. However, this is the compromise that must be taken in order to have a reasonable trade-off between anonymity and user convenience requirements.

8.8   Pairing example

Finally, we give an example of how the presented anonymity modes work when two devices not previously known to each other connect and are paired with each other. We assume that the users of the devices have put their devices in private pairable mode and hence that the devices trust each other and will, in addition to creating a shared link key, exchange alias and private addresses. The main steps related to the connection and pairing procedure are illustrated in Figure 8.5. Below, we explain the procedure step by step.

1. The host that is hosting *device A*, sets the device in anonymous mode using a dedicated command.

2. Host A requires authentication and encryption for any devices that the host connects to or is connected with.

3. Device *A* searches for a new device using the Bluetooth inquiry procedure. A new Bluetooth device, here called *device B*, is discovered. Device *A* receives the active *BD_ADDR_B* from device *B*.

4. Device *A* pages device *B* using *BD_ADDR_B*.

5. During the connection setup, device *A* requires authentication. Since no link key is available, a manual pairing where the users enter a pass-key must be performed.

6. Host A requests a pass-key from the user. The user enters the pass-key, which is transferred to the link manager through the HCI.

7. The link manager of device *A* sends a random number to the link manager of device *B*. The random number is used to calculate an initialization key.

8. The link manager of device *B* requests a pass-key from the user through the HCI. The user enters the pass-key, which is returned to the link manager.

9. The link manager of device *B* calculates the initialization key and return an accept LM PDU to device *A*.

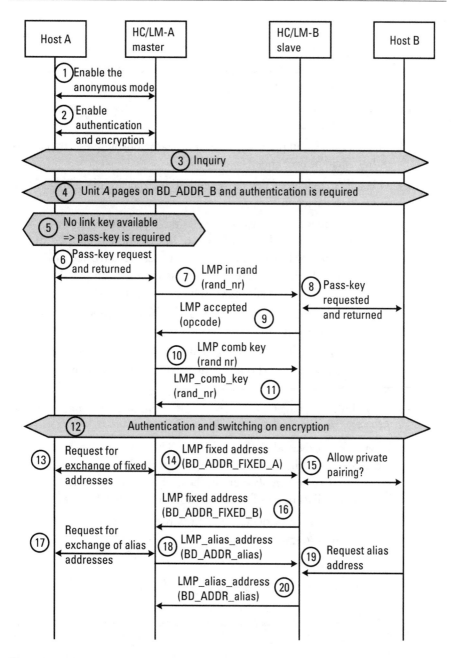

Figure 8.5 Message sequence for pairing with a trusted device.

10. Device *A* generates a random number that is used to calculate a combination key. The random number is sent encrypted with the initialization key to device *B*.

11. Device *B* receives the random number, generates its own random number, which is returned to device *A* encrypted with the initialization key. Both devices decrypt the received random values and calculate the secret combination key.

12. A mutual authentication is performed and the devices switch to encrypted mode.

13. Since device *A* is in private pairable mode, the host requests that a fixed address shall be exchanged.

14. The link manager of device *A* sends the fixed address, *BD_ADDR-fixed_A*, to device *B*.

15. The link manager of device *B* receives the fixed address from *A*. Next, it asks the host if exchange of private information is allowed or not; that is, the host will tell whether or not device *A* is a trusted device that shall receive the fixed address. The host is in private pairable mode. Hence, it accepts fixed addresses to be exchanged.

16. The link manager of device *B* sends the fixed address, *BD_ADDR-fixed_B*, to device *B*.

17. Next, the host of device *A* requests alias addresses to be exchanged and generates an alias that should be used when device *B* identifies device *A*.

18. The link manager of device *A* sends the alias address, *BD_ADDR_alias_A*, to device *B*.

19. Device *B* receives the alias address. The link manager sends the received alias address to the host through the HCI and asks the host for an alias to return. Either the host chooses to use the same alias (symmetric alias) or a different alias (asymmetric alias) is used.

20. The link manager of device *B* returns the alias address for device *B*, *BD_ADDR_alias_B*, to device *A*.

References

[1]   IEEE, *IEEE Standard for Local and Metropolitan Area Networks: Overview and Architecture, IEEE Std. 802-2001*, 2002.

[2]   Bluetooth Special Interest Group, *Specification of the Bluetooth System, Version 1.2, Core System Package*, November 2003.

9

Key Management Extensions

The Bluetooth specification contains the basic tools needed for the creation of security associations and management of security relations. The main key management features are the pairing procedure and update of link keys. The pairing principle with manual assisted key agreement is most suitable for ad hoc creation of security associations. However, in Chapter 7 it was shown that the pairing mechanism is sensitive to off-line and on-line attacks. Hence, there is also a need for alternative, improved pairing solutions. In this chapter, a few of these highly secure pairing procedures are discussed.

Even if the existing pairing principle is nice for ad hoc creation of secure connections, it gives no flexibility in terms of key agreement. It might very well be the case that the user would like to avoid the pairing procedure and instead use preconfigured security associations based on secret or public keys. Then, alternative, widely used standardized key exchange options working on higher layers in the communication stack are the preferred solution. Once a key is agreed upon, the user can choose to use the Bluetooth link layer authentication and encryption or use encryption and/or authentication on higher layers as well. We discuss different key exchange options for higher layers and how they can be combined with the Bluetooth security mechanisms.

Another issue regarding key management in Bluetooth is that devices must always be manually paired before they can communicate securely. In total, one must do as many pairings as there are pairs of devices that are to communicate. Clearly, it can be quite tedious work to perform all these pairings if several devices are involved, which is likely to be the case, for instance, in a domestic domain. This can be avoided by allowing autonomous trust delegation between Bluetooth units. By autonomous trust delegation we mean that security

139

associations are allowed to automatically propagate among trusted devices without any user involvement. Autonomous trust delegation can be achieved using both symmetric and public key techniques, as we will show.

9.1 Improved pairing

The current pairing mechanism has been criticized in several research papers during the last couple of years [1, 2]. Human users tend to use rather short pass-keys (around four digits), and when short pass-keys are used, the pairing mechanism is sensitive to passive eavesdropping or a man-in-the-middle attack. This problem means that there is a need for an alternative solution. In this section we discuss such solutions based on the Diffie-Hellman (DH) [3] key agreement (or exchange). We will describe the details of the DH key exchange in Section 9.1.2. In contrast to the Bluetooth 1.2 pairing mechanism, DH key agreement has the nice property that it is not sensitive to off-line attacks.[1] However, DH key exchange is sensitive to active man-in-the-middle attacks. Consequently, there are a lot of requirements that need to be considered when designing an alternative Bluetooth pairing mechanism. We start this section by discussing requirements of a secure pairing scheme. Next, we present an improved pairing protocol. Finally, the implementation aspects and complexity of the suggested protocol are discussed.

9.1.1 Requirements on an improved pairing protocol

When short pass-keys are used, the current Bluetooth pairing mechanism is vulnerable to both on-line and off-line attacks, as was discussed in Chapter 7. This causes problems for Bluetooth applications with high security requirements. Since manually entering a long pass-key value is not considered to be an acceptable solution, a requirement for an alternative pairing mechanism is that it gives a high security level with as little user involvement as possible. Preferably, this should be achieved with a pairing mechanism similar to the existing one, but secure also for pass-keys of moderate length. The protocol must be secure against the most powerful attack scenario, which implies protection against an active man-in-the-middle attack. Hence, in the DH case there must be some authentication of the key exchange messages.

When one of the devices involved in a pairing does not have any advanced output or input interface (for example, a headset), the only option is to use a fixed pass-key. Then, however, the off-line attack on the Bluetooth 1.2 pairing mechanism is a real threat. This is particularly true when the device without

---

1. This is true also for other public key techniques, such as RSA [4].

sufficient user interface is a stationary device (like an access point or the like), which is an easy target for an attack. Consequently, another requirement for an improved pairing scheme is that it shall also provide sufficient security when a fixed pass-keys are used. It is good security practice to change a fixed pass-key regularly. If the device with a fixed pass-key does not have any proper user interface, this task can be accomplished using some form of a *configuration management* application that communicates with the limited device over a secure interface. One possibility for this is to interface using a secure Bluetooth connection.

It must be possible to implement a solution with low cost. This means that a third requirement of an improved pairing protocol is that it must not be too complex. At the end of this section, we discuss implementation complexity aspects of the suggested improved pairing protocols.

To summarize, the requirements of the pairing protocol are that it have the ability to use *short pass-keys* and *fixed pass-keys*, and that it have *acceptable complexity* demands on the implementation requirements.

9.1.2 Improved pairing protocol

The Bluetooth pairing procedure is actually a *user-assisted* method to create a shared secret between two units. User assistance has the advantage that it is possible to have some level of confidence that the key is exchanged with the expected device and not with a malicious one. What one tries to accomplish with the user interaction is actually the authentication of a key exchange. Henceforth, when alternative, improved pairing proposals are discussed, a user-assisted method is referred to as *manual authentication* (MANA). Manual authentication methods were mentioned by Satjano and Anderson in [5], but they do not consider such methods to be especially user friendly. In particular, they discussed the usage of DH-based key exchange and computed a hash value of the results in both devices. The hash values can then be displayed to the users, who then compare them. There also exist alternative solutions, such as that proposed by Maher [6]. This approach uses short (around 4 to 6 hexadecimal digits) check values and a special implementation of the DH key exchange protocol, where the participants split their DH tokens in two, approximately equally long halves, and fully transmit the first half before transmitting the second half. However, users often tend to accept everything they see on a display, so such methods do not give especially high security. Furthermore, not all Bluetooth devices do actually have a display. Hence, some other MANA solution is desirable.

We will describe a MAC and a DH-based pairing protocol. This protocol was first presented in the European Union (EU) project SHAMAN [7]. The SHAMAN project did a quite extensive study of different security initialization procedures for short-range wireless communication, and the results directly apply to Bluetooth. Alternative DH-based protocols like the SHAKE protocol, which was first proposed at the Open Group conference in Amsterdam 2001 [8], also exist. However, we regard the SHAMAN proposal as the currently available technique that most completely covers the requirements listed in Section 9.1.1.

MAC-based protocol

First, we recall the DH key exchange protocol [9]. The DH key agreement protocol allows two arbitrary entities to agree on a secret key using any available communication channel. The advantage of the protocol is that no information of the other party must be available before the protocol exchange takes place. Several different variants of DH key agreement exist [9]. Here we describe the original using a multiplicative group of integers denoted by Z_p [10]. In the protocol description below, we use A and B, respectively, to denote the two entities involved in the key agreement:

1. An appropriate prime number p and generator g of Z_p (where $2 \leq g \leq p - 2$) are selected and published.

2. A chooses a random secret a, $1 \leq a \leq p-2$, and sends $g^a \bmod p$ to B.

3. B chooses a random secret b, $1 \leq b \leq p-2$, and sends $g^b \bmod p$ to A.

4. A and B calculate the common shared secret, $K = (g^b)^a \bmod p = (g^a)^b \bmod p$.

Now, we will describe how to use manual interaction to make sure that the DH public values, $g^a \bmod p$ and $g^b \bmod p$, come from a legitimate source. The protocol is divided into two separate parts, stage I and stage II. The first stage can be done in advance, while the second stage is executed when the actual key exchange takes place. Manual interaction is only necessary during stage I. The latter is an advantage of the suggested protocol. In principle, one of the units creates a set of secret parameters at stage I to use in the key agreement protocol. Some of these are needed by the other unit at stage II, so they must be transferred to it in some way. These parameters constitute a secret pass-key.

This is a one-way transaction, which does have some implications. First, it means that it is possible to do the transaction off-line. For instance, the necessary parameters could be sent by mail when one is registering for a particular service for which Bluetooth access points are used. Naturally, there is nothing that prevents the two steps from being performed in sequence directly after each other, and this will probably be the typical usage. Secondly, the source must have a way of presenting the parameters to the world, while the destination must have a way of entering the parameters. These requirements are most likely translated into a display and keyboard, respectively. Thus, this method can be utilized for pairing with Bluetooth equipment having a display, but without any proper input device (e.g., access points, headsets).

The protocol is not completely symmetric and the units involved in the pairing need to take either the role of device *A* or device *B*. The demand on the user interface for the two roles is slightly different. Device *A* must at least have a user interface to present a secret pass-key, and device *B* must at least have a user interface to input the corresponding pass-key. Which role to take can be negotiated during the pairing.

Next, the MAC-based pairing protocol will be described. For the moment, we do not define the MAC function, but it is assumed that devices *A* and *B* share one. A proposal and detailed analysis of the properties of the MAC function can be found in Section 9.1.2. Figure 9.1 illustrates the different protocol steps that are outlined below. In this description, the received variables and values derived directly from these are marked with a prime (′) in order to distinguish them from values generated from locally stored variables.

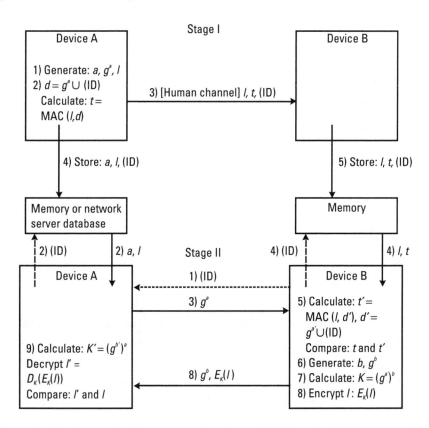

Figure 9.1 The improved pairing protocol based on a MAC function. The parameter ID is optional (marked with surrounding parentheses).

Stage I

1. Device A generates a and the corresponding DH key g^a and a short secret string in any suitable format, l.

2. Device A uses a MAC to calculate a message tag, t. The input to the MAC is g^a and possibly some other data (for example, an identifier, ID). The key used to calculate the tag t is the secret string l.

3. Through direct human interaction, registration, or other means, the secret value consisting of l and t together with an optional identifier, ID, are given to device B.

4. Device A stores in internal memory or in a network database the values a, l, and, if applicable, the ID.

5. Device B stores in internal memory or in a network database the values l, t, and, if applicable, the ID.

Stage II

1. Device B would like to make a secure connection to device A (or to some access point acting on behalf of the network server that generated the secret a). Device B initiates the key agreement with device A, optionally by transmitting the ID.

2. Device A finds the secret key, a, and the corresponding secret MAC key, l, to be used (using the received ID', if available).

3. Device A calculates and sends g^a to device B.

4. Device B finds the l and t (corresponding to the ID).

5. Device B calculates the MAC t' of the received $g^{a'}$ and possibly some other data using the secret string l. If $t = t'$, the public key $g^{a'}$ is accepted.

6. Device B generates a second DH key b and the corresponding DH key g^b.

7. Device B calculates the DH shared secret, $K = (g^{a'})^b$.

8. Device B uses the key K to encrypt the string l using some arbitrary secure encryption function and sends g^b and the encrypted l to device A.

9. Device A receives $g^{b'}$ and the encrypted l string. Device A derives the DH key $K' = (g^{b'})^a$ and decrypts the l' using the key K'. If l' matches the stored string, l, then K' is accepted as a shared secret between A and B.

Obviously, one can think of several different variants of this basic protocol. In the Bluetooth 1.2 specification, there is no built-in support for the

MAC-based pairing protocol, but future versions may incorporate it. It is possible, though, to implement an improved pairing at higher layers and pass the agreed-on link key to the Bluetooth through the HCI. We discuss different implementation options in Section 9.1.3.

One advantage of the MAC-based pairing is that the authentication values are not revealed in the authentication exchange, so it is possible to use them more than once. This property is a significant improvement compared to the Bluetooth 1.2 pairing method, where the fixed pass-key value is not secure. For example, this can be utilized by a device that does not have any good input or output interface (like an access point or a headset). Then a fixed pass-key value is often the only option to use, and we would like to be able to use the same pass-key for several consecutive pairings without compromising security. The main drawback with the protocol is that it requires that public key operations be supported in both devices. Hence, it might not be suitable to use for all kinds of Bluetooth devices.

MAC construction and security of the protocol

In order to achieve high security with the short MAC key, l, and tag value, t, the MAC codes used in the enhanced protocol must be constructed in a certain way. We consider the best choice to combine a secure one-way hash function like SHA-1 [11] and an unconditionally secure message authentication code [12]. Such a code can be constructed in a practical way from codes with large minimum distance, such as the Reed-Solomon codes (RS-codes) [13], as was shown in [7] and which we briefly describe here.

In general, a MAC is a mapping from a message and key space to a tag space. We use $\mathscr{D}$, $\mathscr{L}$, and $\mathscr{T}$, respectively, to denote the message, key, and tag space. Thus,

$$\mathrm{MAC}\colon \mathscr{D} \times \mathscr{L} \to \mathscr{T}, \quad (d,l) \mapsto t \qquad (9.1)$$

We recall that the input message, d, is g^a and possibly some other data, such as an identifier. The key, l, is the short random string to be given (possibly through a display) to the user and should be entered into one device according to the proposed pairing procedure.

RS-codes can be described using a polynomial representation. This representation is most suitable for description and implementation of MACs based on RS-codes, and we use it also for our description. The code is constructed using an arbitrary finite field. A finite field is a finite set with two binary operators, $+$ and $\cdot$, defined on the elements in the set. In addition, a certain set of axioms must hold in order for the system (the set including the operators on the elements) to be a finite field [14]. We use q to denote the size of the field (i.e., the field contains q elements) and $\mathbf{F}_q$ to denote the corresponding field. One example of a field of size p is the set of integers, $\{0, 1, \ldots, p-1\}$, where p is a prime number and where we define addition, $+$, and multiplication, $\cdot$, operations as addition and multiplication modulo p.

Using the introduced terminology and notations, we are now able to describe the MAC construction itself. We use h to denote an (arbitrary) one-way hash function, such as SHA-1. First, the hash function is used to reduce the original message, d, to a smaller message, $m = h(d)$, which is more suitable to use as input to the RS-code-based MAC. Next, the hash is written as a q-ary sequence of length n, that is, $m = m_0, m_1, \ldots, m_{n-1}, m_i \in \mathbf{F}_q$. Then the MAC for the key $l \in \mathbf{F}_q$ and data d is given by

$$\mathrm{MAC}(l, d) = m_0 + m_1 l + m_2 l^2 + \ldots + m_{n-1} l^{n-1} \qquad (9.2)$$

The (l, t) key-tag pair of the MAC protocol can be seen as the equivalent of the pass-key of ordinary Bluetooth pairing. The same user-operated pass-key value can be used more than once, but must be kept secret as long as it is going to be used for pairing. Any party in possession of a valid key l is able to impersonate a device that uses a fixed pass-key. Hence, the fixed pass-key value should be updated as often as possible to increase security. Since we use DH key agreement as the basis for the key exchange protocol, a revealed pass-key will not cause any danger to keys derived from previous pairings.

One DH public key can remain constant. This can be used in a network access scenario to simplify key agreement with several different users. It is also possible to allow both DH public values to remain constant, but then a fresh random value should be included into the key derivation function. The DH group parameters can be chosen in different ways. The straightforward choice is to use a multiplicative group over the integers. But other choices such as DH over an elliptic curve [14] is also possible.

The security of the protocol depends on the length of the pass-key, that is, the MAC key and MAC tag values, the security of the DH protocol, the hash function, and the MAC function. An analysis of the security is presented in [7]. A requirement is that the DH key agreement and the one-way hash function are computationally secure. When this is true, the risk of off-line attacks on the pairing is eliminated and the security of the scheme depends solely on the length of the pass-key value. The most powerful attack that remains is an active man-in-the-middle attack, where, given a DH public key, the attacker must find another DH key with the same tag value, t, without knowledge of l and t.

Table 9.1 lists the probabilities for successful man-in-the-middle attack on the improved pairing protocol. In the table it is assumed that RS-code-based MAC construction is used. From Table 9.1, one can see that the probability

Table 9.1
RS-Code MAC Construction Examples with Probability for Successful Man-in-the-Middle Attack

Size of Message Hash	Pass-Key Size (Decimal Digits)	Pass-Key Size (Bytes)	Probability of Successful Attack
128	5	2	$< 2^{-4}$
128	8	3	$< 2^{-8}$
128	10	4	$< 2^{-13}$
256	10	4	$< 2^{-12}$
128	12	5	$< 2^{-17}$
256	12	5	$< 2^{-16}$

rapidly decreases with increased pass-key size for the chosen MAC. For small pass-key sizes like 2 bytes (5 decimal digits), the probability of a successful man-in-the-middle attack is less than 1/16. For most applications, a pass-key size of 4 bytes (10 decimal digits) provides a reasonable security level.

9.1.3 Implementation aspects and complexity

In order to support the improved pairing procedure, there must be a transport protocol for transferring the key exchange messages. Currently, the Bluetooth specification does not contain any built-in support for the DH key exchange. Hence, no standard compliant implementation of a DH-based protocol can be implemented at the LMP level. There are several different higher layer candidates, though. When we look into the existing Bluetooth profiles, the most attractive candidates are the OBEX [15] or the PAN profile [16]. When using the PAN profile, several different possibilities exist. TCP is one rather natural choice. Another nice possible option in the PAN case would be to have it defined as the Internet Engineering Task Force (IETF) *extensible authentication protocol* (EAP) [17] mechanism and use the IEEE 802.1x port-based network access control framework [18]. We will discuss IEEE 802.1x in detail in Section 9.2, and we restrict the description here to the OBEX and TCP alternatives. Figure 9.2 illustrates the placement of the improved pairing protocol for the OBEX variant and Figure 9.3 shows the same thing for the PAN/TCP option.

From a protocol and usability point of view, there is no major difference between the two options, and other variants are possible as well. Independent of the chosen protocol solution, in order to be combined with the ordinary link security mechanisms, the agreed-on link key must be stored in the key database of the device. One can use the DH key as a long pass-key input to the "ordinary"

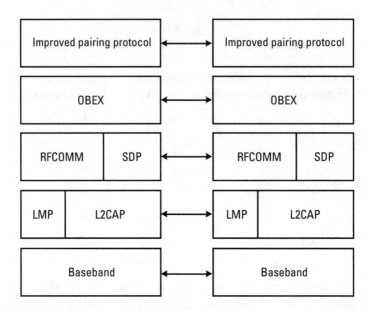

Figure 9.2 The protocol stack and the placement of the improved pairing protocol using the OBEX option.

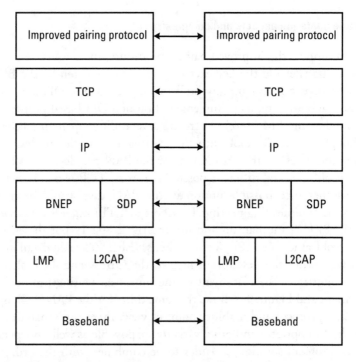

Figure 9.3 The protocol stack and the placement of the improved pairing protocol using the PAN/TCP option.

pairing, or use it directly as the link key. The latter approach is preferable, being straightforward and less complex. There must then be a mapping between the agreed-on key (derived from the DH key) and the device address (or in the case of anonymity mode, the alias address of the other device). If the key database resides on the host, in the nonanonymous case, the address can be obtained using the HCI command `HCI Read BD_ADDR`. In the anonymous case, the alias address is generated when the devices pair in *private pairable mode* (see Chapter 8). Hence, in this case, alias addresses needs to be exchanged after the improved pairing.

If the improved pairing is implemented on higher layers as in the two options we have discussed, then it is not possible to use security mode 3. This is because, in security mode 3, the pairing is initiated before a connection has been set up, and the units are not able to exchange any information at a higher layer. However, an improved pairing protocol implemented at a higher layer works fine with security mode 2. In that case, both units must be configured not to initiate any security procedures until an OBEX or TCP channel (PAN case) has been established. If security should be maintained, it is important that the implementation only allows the pairing protocol to run over the OBEX or TCP transport until the other device is authenticated.

Using the suggested improved pairing with a DH key agreement over a large integer prime order group causes considerable increase in bandwidth compared to the Bluetooth 1.2 pairing mechanism. If this is considered a problem, other DH groups are available. The most suitable to use in that case would be Elliptic-Curve Diffie-Hellman (ECDH) [14]. Using ECDH, the key exchange can be implemented in software with quite a small footprint for the protocol. For an elliptic curve over a field of around 2^{160} in size (i.e., with the underlying field size of 160 bits), we have a public key size also of about 160 bits (20 bytes). This implies that not more than 20 bytes of key information need to be sent (in each direction) over the radio channel at the pairing. The choice of elliptic curve parameters can be of any standard type like the one proposed by the IEEE 1363 group [19] or ANSI X9.63 [20].

9.2 Higher layer key exchange

So far we have only discussed a particular pass-key-based alternative to the Bluetooth 1.2 pairing mechanism. Pass-key-based solutions fit well into situations where connections are created ad hoc and under control by people. However, in several different situations, this is not the case. Sometimes, we would like to be able to create Bluetooth link keys fully automatically without any user interaction at all. In this section we discuss a couple of such approaches, showing how the methods can be implemented in combination with the existing Bluetooth security mechanisms. Higher layer key exchange for Bluetooth was first presented by Blake-Wilson in [21].

As in Section 9.1, some methods for the establishment of a unique, strong shared secret data item between two Bluetooth devices will be discussed. Clearly, this data item can be directly used as a combination link key and, thus, can be stored in the link key database of the host or module (the one applicable). Alternatively, it can be used as a high-entropy Bluetooth pass-key in the ordinary Bluetooth 1.2 pairing procedure. However, if the higher layer key exchange is used, there is no extra benefit of using the shared secret as a pass-key for conventional pairing compared to using it as the link key.

The IEEE 801.1x [18] authentication and key exchange framework defines several different authentication options for LAN and wireless local area network (WLAN) systems. This framework utilizes EAP [17] for the transfer of authentication information. The EAP has been standardized by the IETF as a protocol to support multiple authentication mechanisms by encapsulating the messages used by the different authentication methods. Since IEEE 801.1x is defined over Ethernet frames, it can be used in Bluetooth directly on the Bluetooth Network Encapsulation Protocol (BNEP) [22], which is part of the PAN profile [16]. This fact and the flexibility and wide support of the IEEE 801.1x framework make it most useful also for Bluetooth applications. The higher layer key exchange mechanisms to be described here are based on ideas and concepts from the IEEE 802.1x. The authenticated key exchange methods supported are, for example, Kerberos [23], TLS [24], and even a pass-key protocol. For example, one can think of defining an EAP variant of the protocol we described in Section 9.1. The list of supported IEEE 802.1x authentication methods is expected to grow to accommodate future needs. Many of these authentication schemes produce session key material that in our setting can be used as the strong shared secret data item.

9.2.1   IEEE 802.1x port-based network access control

In this section we first give a brief introduction to the IEEE 802.1x authentication framework. Next, we address how these ideas can be used in Bluetooth, and finally we focus on some exemplary higher layer key exchange mechanisms.

In IEEE 802.1x, the term *port* is used for a point of attachment to a LAN, and the standard defines mechanisms for *port-based network access*. The term refers to the fact that until a peer has been successfully authenticated and authorized, all services on the other peer except the authentication service itself are locked—the port is closed. Once the peer is successfully authenticated, the LAN port is opened and the peer is granted access to the authorized services. Three different roles are defined in the standard:

1. The *Authenticator* is the port that wants to authenticate the connecting device before allowing access to services provided by that port.

2. The *Supplicant* is the connecting device that tries to access some service provided by the port.

3. The *Authentication server* provides the actual authentication function, that is, verifies the identity of the peer and performs the necessary cryptographic operations needed to make the verification.

Typically, one does not need to separate the authenticator and authenticator server roles—they may well be colocated on the same physical device. However, in a network access case, it makes sense to have the actual verification performed on a dedicated network server that can serve several different access points (the ports). The authenticator makes use of two ports: an *uncontrolled port* for authentication messages and a *controlled port* for the subsequent connection. The controlled port does not let any traffic through until there is successful authentication over the uncontrolled port.

In IEEE 802.1x, the actual authentication is based on EAP. EAP defines several different mechanisms and IEEE 802.1x can be used with any of them. The EAP packets are encapsulated in Ethernet frames as defined by the standard. The EAP messages are transferred between the supplicant and the authentication server. If the authentication server is a special device separated from the authenticator, the authenticator only acts as a pass-through for the EAP messages. Once the authentication has been finalized, the authenticator gets information of the outcome through the *EAP-success* or *EAP-failure* messages.

When IEEE 802.1x is used in Bluetooth, the supplicant role can be taken by the paging device, while the role of the authenticator can be taken by the paged device (think of an access point scenario). The authentication server is either located directly in the paged device or implemented as a backed server. This will be application dependent and is no different from the LAN usage case. The EAP packets are encapsulated in Ethernet frames using BNEP, defined in the Bluetooth PAN profile. Figure 9.4 illustrates the encapsulation principles. IEEE 802.1x uses the EAP encapsulation over LANs (EAPOL) frame format when carrying EAP information over Ethernet. In addition to transferring pure EAP messages, EAPOL also carries some signaling messages and is used to transport keys.

Since the EAP messages only can be exchanged once a BNEP connection has been established, it is not possible for Bluetooth to use IEEE 802.1x directly together with security mode 3. This follows from the fact that security mode 3 requires the security procedures to be run before the link setup is completed. Then the authentication (and encryption) protocol(s) must use the legacy methods provided by the specification. However, security mode 2 fits nicely together

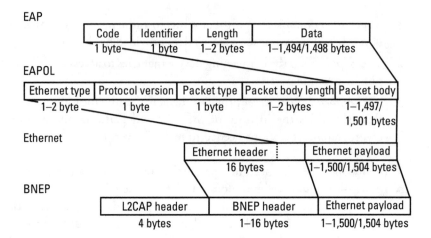

Figure 9.4 Frame formats when using BENEP and IEEE 802.1x to perform EAP authentication in Bluetooth.

with the IEEE 802.1x framework. Once the authentication has been performed, a link key based upon the authentication exchange will be looked up in the key database of each device. When this is retrieved, conventional authentication (which is a prerequisite to baseband encryption) and optionally encryption can be performed.

9.2.2 Higher layer key exchange with EAP TLS

In the following we present an exemplary EAP mechanism, namely the TLS [25] protocol, which has been defined as an EAP mechanism [24]. TLS, which is similar to other EAP authentication methods, produces session key material that in our setting can be used to establish the strong shared secret data item. TLS is a well-known and widely used protocol, which provides communications privacy, including authentication between two devices and exchange of cryptographic keys. It is designed to prevent eavesdropping, tampering, and message forgery. Thus, TLS can be used to implement higher layer key exchange in Bluetooth.

TLS has several different options for authentication and algorithm choices. Figure 9.5 shows one typical successful EAP-TLS message sequence, with successful TLS server and client authentication (mutual authentication). One of the Bluetooth units must take the IEEE 802.1x authenticator role and the other unit the supplicant role. Even if this is "normally" done in order to authorize access to a port, for most Bluetooth applications we would only use the EAP messages for authentication and key exchange. The message exchange sequence starts with the slave unit requesting authentication through the EAPOL-Start message. Next, the authenticator requests an identity from the supplicant unit. Once this

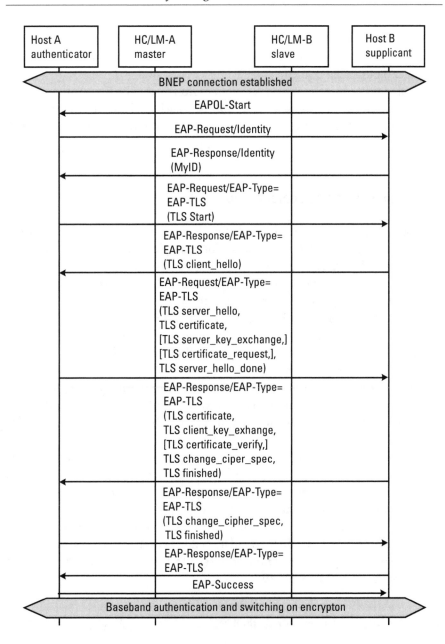

Figure 9.5 EAP-TLS message sequence example.

identity is given, the TLS protocol exchange takes place. For details of the TLS protocol, we refer to [25]. The successful TLS handshake is confirmed by the authenticator through the EAP-success message. Following a successful key exchange, the agreed-on TLS master secret should be used as the link key for the connections and the units should perform an ordinary baseband authentication using the master secret obtained from the successful EAP mutual authentication. This is also illustrated in the message sequence diagram.

Obviously, another option is to refrain from using the Bluetooth link level security at all, and instead use another protocol such as IPsec [26, 27] to protect the communication between the units once the units have exchanged the master secret.

9.3   Autonomous trust delegation

Bluetooth pairing mechanisms might cause unnecessarily numerous pairings when a user has several PAN devices. For example, when having a group of devices we will have as many manual pairings as there are pairs of devices that want to communicate. However, this can be avoided if we allow security associations to be propagated between devices through a security group extension method. In this section we will describe and discuss two such methods. The first method is based on the propagation of group keys. With the use of the suggested method, the number of manual parings in a PAN of n devices is reduced from $n(n-1)/2$ to a number between $n-1$ and $n(n-1)/2$, depending on the order in which the users perform the pairings. The second approach is to use public keys and public key certificates in order to improve key management. The idea is to let one dedicated, trusted Bluetooth unit certify public keys of all trusted units in a certain group of units. The certified keys can then be used for key exchange between all trusted units in the group. Security group extension methods can be achieved though a combination of ordinary Bluetooth pairing in combination with trust delegation. The pairing can be the ordinary pairing method or the new, improved pairing mechanism that we described in Section 9.1.

The key management extension methods presented in this section are briefly described in [28]. In particular, public key–based key management, called the personal *public key infrastructure* (PKI), has been extensively treated in the EU project SHAMAN [7, 29].

9.3.1   Security group extension method

By *trust delegation* we mean that trust relations are allowed to autonomously propagate among Bluetooth devices through new pairings between the devices. One could argue that this causes trust to be spread in an uncontrolled manner among a huge set of devices. However, this can be avoided with correct handling of the pairings on a user level. Here we describe the solution for trust delegation based on symmetric keys. Another approach for automatic trust delegation is public key–based key management, which we treat in Section 9.3.2.

According to our proposed method, each device supporting the trust delegation method has an internal trusted group key database. The database contains a list with at least the following two entries for each record:

1. A group key index;
2. A secret key corresponding to the index.

Each device might be preconfigured by the manufacturer with at least one key index chosen at random and a corresponding group key. Alternatively, it is shipped with no group key at all. When the user would like to connect two devices (that have not previously been in contact with each other), here called the first and second devices, the following procedure applies:

1. The first device requests a pairing of the two devices. If the second device refuses this request, the procedure is aborted. If the second device accepts the request for pairing, the next step applies.

2. The devices decide whether a group key–based pairing or a conventional pairing is going to take place. This can be accomplished by specifically asking the user to authorize (or reject) a group key–based pairing, or proceed according to device-specific security settings regarding this issue. If a conventional pairing is chosen, the next step is 6; otherwise the next step is 3.

3. The first device sends the list of key indexes from its group key database to the second device. If the group key database is empty, this fact shall be made known to the second unit.

4. The second device receives the list of indexes and checks the list against the internal list of trusted group key indexes. If the device finds a match between any of the received indexes and the internally stored list of indexes, the device chooses an arbitrary index among the matches and returns this index to the first device, and the procedure continues with step 5. If no match is found, the second device returns an indication to the first device that nothing matched and whether or not its own list is empty, and then step 6 is performed.

5. The two devices perform an authenticated key exchange. The authentication is based on the group key corresponding to the agreed-on index. The authenticated key exchange can, for example, be the ordinary Bluetooth pairing procedure with the group key used as pass-key. The next step is 8.

6. The two devices perform a manual pairing. This can be an ordinary pairing or an improved one, as we described in Section 9.1. A group

key pairing shall only be performed if the user confirms that the devices regard each other as "highly trusted." If a group key–based pairing is to be performed, the procedure continues with step 7. If a conventional pairing is taking place, the procedure ends here.

7. If both devices' lists are empty, the second device generates a group key and a corresponding key index, both uniformly and randomly chosen. The key and index can be of any size, but a 128-bit group key size and a 48-bit key index, for example, are the most suitable for the Bluetooth system. The procedure continues with the next step.

8. The two devices switch to an encrypted connection using the recently agreed-on secret key.

9. The second device calculates what items the first device is missing from the second device's list of trusted group key indexes and corresponding keys. These items are sent to the first device, which will add all previously unknown indexes and keys to its own trusted key database.

10. The first device calculates what items the second device is missing from the first device's list of trusted group key indexes and corresponding keys. These items are sent to the second device, which will add all previously unknown indexes and keys to its own trusted key database. This ends the procedure.

This procedure is repeated at each pairing occasion. Whenever two devices regard each other as "highly trusted," they will exchange trusted group keys. This allows trust relations to propagate among the devices. This in turn will considerably reduce the number of manual pairings needed when several devices are going to be paired with each other.

An example

Next we give an example of how the group extension method works when only four devices are involved in the trust delegation. Let A, B, C, and D denote the four different devices. In the example, we have assumed that the devices are not preconfigured with any group key from the start. Below we describe the four different pairing steps. The steps are illustrated in Figures 9.6 and 9.7.

1. Two devices, A and B, are connected for the first time. No trusted group keys are stored in any of the devices and they perform a manual pairing based on a pass-key. Both users indicate that this is a pairing with a highly trusted device, and after authentication and a switch to encryption, device A generates a trusted group key with index 1^2 and sends this index and key to B. Both devices store the trusted group key K_1 in their respective databases.

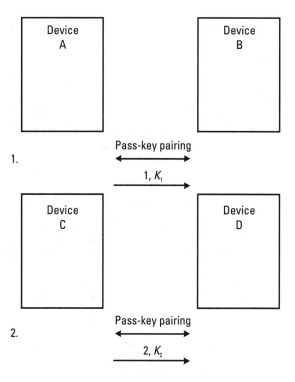

Figure 9.6 Trusted group extension example, steps 1 and 2.

2. Two devices, *C* and *D*, are connected for the first time. No trusted group keys are stored in any of the devices and they perform a manual pairing based on pass-keys entered into both devices. Both users indicate that this is a pairing with a highly trusted device, and after authentication and a switch to encryption, device *C* generates a trusted group key with index 2 and sends this index and key to *D*. Both devices store the trusted group key K_2 in their respective databases.

3. Two devices, *A* and *C*, are connected for the first time. Device *A* sends the index of its only trusted group key, number 1, to device *C*. *C* has no key with index 1 and replies with a request for bonding. The devices perform a manual pairing based on a pass-key. Both users indicate that this is a bonding with a highly trusted device, and after authentication and a switch to encryption, device *A* sends its list of trusted group keys, that is, index 1 and key K_1 to device *C*. *C* replies with its list of trusted group keys, that is, index 2 and key K_2. Device A

---

2. The index should be chosen from a large space to avoid collisions. In order to simplify the description, we here just choose the indexes 1, 2, 3, and so on.

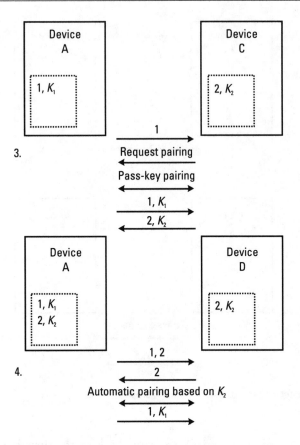

Figure 9.7 Trusted group extension example, steps 3 and 4.

stores the new group key K_2 in its database and device C stores the new group key K_1 in its database.

4. Two devices, A and D, are connected for the first time. Device A sends the index of its trusted group keys, that is, 1 and 2, to device C. C has a key index 2 in its trusted group key database and replies with key index 2. The devices perform an authenticated key exchange based on K_2. After authentication and a switch to encryption, device A sends the trusted group keys with index 1 and the key K_1 to device D. D does not have any additional trusted group keys and just accepted the last index and key.

Implementation aspects

The trusted group extension approach can be used without the improved pairing proposal in Section 9.1 (even if the security is not as high as with it).

Together with improved pairing, it gives higher security, and, if desired, it can provide functionality similar to the public key–based key management methods we will describe in Section 9.3.2. This is achieved if personal devices are always first paired with one particular device. The trusted group extension can be implemented independently of the security modes, and the only requirement is that it is possible to distinguish between a pairing with a highly trusted device and other situations. It must then be possible on the user interface level to make the distinction between highly trusted devices and other devices.

The trusted group extension requires a slightly modified pairing protocol to be used. As with the improved pairing proposal, we have several options on where to implement the support for the new protocol. The ideal case would be to introduce a set of new LMP commands for this purpose. However, this requires changes to the Bluetooth specification or the use of proprietary Bluetooth modules with this functionality. If this is not a possible option, the protocol can be implemented according to the principles we discussed for the improved pairing protocol in Section 9.1.3. That is, using OBEX or defining a new IETF EAP for this purpose. The most attractive solution from a pure security point of view is to offer the trusted group extension as part of the improved pairing functionality.

Introducing several security groups

The trusted group extension method can be used to propagate trust relations among units in an ad hoc fashion. So far, we have only considered trust propagation for one uniform group. The trust relations can only be extended within this single group. If only one group is allowed, there is a risk that this group is extended rapidly without control. If this happens, the security of the system is compromised. Hence, it must always be possible for the user to reset the trusted group key database (and possibly the link key derived in this group) of the device, and in that way damage can be avoided. Thus, for the group extension method to be secure, the user must be very careful with extending the security group. Furthermore, in some scenarios we would like to create, for example, temporary groups or groups with different rights. Then, in order to maintain a good security level, one must allow several different groups to be created. Each group can be created with a special purpose and with certain security limitations. For example, one can limit the lifetime of the group and/or the security policy for the members of that group. This can be done in accordance with the PAN security domain ideas introduced in [7].

Supporting several different security groups creates additional requirements. Group key indexes and the link keys obtained from pairings or key exchange in a group must be stored together or must be marked. Furthermore, a user-friendly name should be associated with the group. It is only when manual pairing applies that the user must be involved in choosing the right group. On the protocol level there, it must be possible to deal with the different groups and group extensions for the different groups. This means, for instance, that each group must be authenticated separately, before the group keys should be spread. We do not deal with the detailed requirements or solutions for supporting several security groups here, but leave the details of such solutions to people interested in implementing such a feature.

9.3.2   Public key–based key management

The basic idea behind trust delegation was to allow units to communicate securely without necessarily requiring manual pairing for each pair of communicating Bluetooth units. Similar features can be achieved with a public key–based key management scheme for Bluetooth. The ideas for public key–based key management that we describe here originate from work done by the EU project SHAMAN [7, 29]. Work related to this concept has also been published in [30].

In a conventional PKI, a *certificate authority* (CA) issues a public key certificate like those following the X.509 standard format [31]. The CA is responsible for checking that the public key in a certificate corresponds to a private key that the holder (with the ID given in the certificate) of the certificate possesses. This is necessary in order to maintain the security of a global or a very large PKI. The drawbacks are that a central CA must issue all necessary certificates used by the communication units and the users of the units must get in direct contact with the CA if a high security level should be achieved. This might be a tedious process that a user of a communication unit would like to avoid. Furthermore, it is very costly to maintain a well-controlled, highly secure certification process that can handle thousands of users. On the other hand, users that might want to operate their own local environment, such as a Bluetooth network, have no benefits inside their local network from having a centralized CA. In addition, users might not want, for privacy reasons, to delegate the CA operation to a centralized entity outside their personal environment.

To avoid the drawbacks with the centralized CA that we mentioned above, one can instead introduce the CA role in the local Bluetooth network. That means that one of the Bluetooth units in the network takes the certification issuing role. Such a unit is a *personal certification device* (PCD). A PCD is used to certify all of one's Bluetooth units and equip them with mutually trusted public key certificates. This means that each device utilizing the PCD must have public key capability and have its public key certified by the PCD before it can be used for authentication or key management purposes. The PCD might be preconfigured (by the manufacturer) with a private-public key pair. Alternatively, it must be able to generate such a key pair. The personal PCD device is used to initialize other personal communication devices. In order to illustrate the principle, we will give an example of how the certification and key management can work when using a PCD:

A user buys a new Bluetooth-enabled mobile phone. The mobile phone has the capability to act as a PCD in a Bluetooth network and the user decides to use the phone as a certification device. Hence, the user activates the PCD functionality in the mobile phone.

At a later point in time, the user decides to buy two more Bluetooth-capable devices, say a laptop and a printer. We assume that the user wants to make the new devices part of a set of trusted devices. This is done using an initialization procedure.

The initialization means that the user needs to connect the new devices, that is, the laptop and the printer, with the PCD. (We will discuss in detail how such an initialization will work.)

During the initialization, the PCD issues public key certificates to the two new devices and transfers a common trusted root key to them.

Once the laptop and the printer have the trusted root key and their certificates, they will be able to set up secure connections without user involvement with all other devices belonging to the same PCD. Hence, it will be possible for the laptop to connect to the printer, verify the identity of the printer, automatically pair with the printer and exchange a common link key, and then securely communicate with the printer.

From the description above, one can see that there are two main functions needed in order to support a key management architecture based on public key certificates from a PCD:

1. An initialization procedure;
2. Authentication and key exchange based on public key certificates.

Next we will discuss the details of these two functions.

Initialization procedure

The first thing to do when adding a new device to a personal network is to connect the new device to the PCD. Next, the PCD will equip the connecting device with a public key certificate and the public root key that can be used to verify certificates issued by the PCD. One can think of several different ways to do the initialization. Below we give a step-by-step description of one possible procedure, where A denotes the connecting device.

1. In the request for a certificate, device A sends its identity together with a public key to the PCD over Bluetooth. In order to proof the

possession of the private key corresponding to the public key, device A should sign the request for a certificate. This signed request might, for example, be according to the PKCS #10 standard [32].

2. The PCD replies by sending its own public root key to device A.

3. Device A needs to authenticate the PCD public root key. Similarly, the PCD needs to authenticate the public key of device A. This can be done using a variant of the MAC-based manual authentication procedure described in Section 9.1.2 by replacing the public DH values (if non-DH public keys are used) with the public keys of device A and the PCD, respectively.

4. The PCD issues a new certificate for device A. The certificate contains (among other information) the identity and public key of device A. All the information to be included in the certificate is digitally signed by the PCD, with the private key corresponding to the public root key sent in step 2. The signature is included in the new certificate.

5. The PCD sends the new certificate to device A.

6. The PCD stores the new certificate. Preferably, the certificate (as well as the root key) is stored in a tamper-resistant memory or securely stored by any other means.

7. Device A stores the new certificate together with the public root key of the PCD in protected memory.

After the initialization has been completed, device A possesses a certificate that it can present to all other devices that have been initialized with the same PCD. The public key in that certificate can be used by the other device to authenticate device A and exchange session keys, as will be described in the next section. The main idea with the public key–based approach using a PCD is that all devices initialized with the same PCD will be in the same security domain. This means that all these devices share a common trusted root, the public root key of the PCD. Hence, all devices will trust all other certificates in the same domain. Normally, in a public key infrastructure with a centralized CA, it must be possible to revoke certificates once a private key is compromised, a device is stolen, or the like. This is in principle also true for the public key–based key management scheme we discuss here. However, as long as the approach is used for a small number of devices (e.g., personal, home, or small office usage), the revocation is not a big problem. If one of the devices in the domain is compromised or stolen, it will be possible for the user to reset the security setting in all remaining devices and just repeat the security initialization with new keys and certificates.

Authentication and key exchange procedure

Possessing trusted certificates is not enough for a complete key management architecture in Bluetooth. There must also be the means for the devices to authenticate each other and exchange keys to be used for encryption. Bluetooth's built-in authentication and encryption mechanisms do not use certificates. Thus, what is primarily needed is an authentication and key exchange procedure based on certificates. The goal with such a procedure would be to equip the devices with a common Bluetooth link key. For this to work, it is required that the public keys in the certificates issued by the PCD can be used for authenticated key exchange. The algorithms and certificate requirement will depend on the protocol used for the authenticated key exchange. In Section 9.2, we discussed different higher layer key exchange procedures. Some of these procedures are certificate based. Hence, they can be used to achieve the authenticated key exchange we need. In particular, we described the TLS-based key exchange in Section 9.2.2. Since TLS also provides integrity and confidentiality protection through message authentication codes and encryption algorithms, TLS is also a good alternative to the Bluetooth link level encryption for communication protection.

9.3.3 Group extension method versus public key method

The trust delegation based on the security group extension method in Section 9.3.1 only reduces the number of manual interactions needed for security association establishment; it does not make manual pairing superfluous. For a group of devices, the number of pairings required depends on the order of the pairings. One cannot require the user to make the pairings in a certain order. Hence, the number of pairings needed for a group with n devices will be between $n-1$ and $n(n-1)/2$. If users always pair their new devices with a certain initialization device, the number of initializations will equal $n-1$. This is the same situation as when the public key–based key management described in Section 9.3.2 is used. According to these principles, all security initialization is done with the PCD. However, in that case the user has no other choice than to pair each device with the PCD and only a small number of pairing orders are possible. This particular pairing order corresponds to an optimal pairing order using the security group extension method. While this speaks in favor of public key–based key management, there are also drawbacks. The PCD must always be present when a security initialization is performed. Furthermore, the PCD approach can only be used when public keys are supported by the Bluetooth devices. In the secure group extension method, no device has any particular role, and any device can be used to delegate the trust relation to any other device. Moreover, the trust delegation method can be accomplished with only minor extensions to the standard Bluetooth pairing, which is not the case for the PCD-based approach.

References

[1]   Kügler, D., "Man in the Middle Attacks on Bluetooth," revised papers, in R. N. Wright, ed., *Financial Cryptography, 7th International Conf., FC 2003*, Guadeloup, No. 2742 in LNCS, Springer-Verlag, 2003, pp. 149–61.

[2]   Jakobsson, M., and S. Wetzel, "Security Weaknesses in Bluetooth," in D. Naccache, (ed.), *Proc. RSA Conf. 2001*, No. 2020 in LNCS, San Francisco: Springer-Verlag, April 8–12, 2001.

[3]   Diffie, W., and M. E. Hellman, "New Directions in Cryptography," *IEEE Trans. Information Theory*, Vol. 22, 1976, pp. 644–654.

[4]   Shamir, A., R. L. Rivest, and L. Adleman, "A Method for Obtaining Digital Signatures and Public Key Cryptosystems," *Comm. ACM*, Vol. 21, 1978, pp. 294–299.

[5]   Stajano, F., and R. Anderson, "The Resurrecting Duckling: Security Issues for ad-hoc Wireless Networks," *Security Protocols, 7th International Workshop*, No. 1796 in LNCS, Cambridge: Springer-Verlag, April 1999.

[6]   Maher, D., "Secure Communication Method and Apparatus," U.S. Patent No. 5,450,492, 1995.

[7]   Sovio, S., et al. "D13, Annex 2, Specification of a Security Architecture for Distributed Terminals," Report IST-2000-25250, IST project SHAMAN, 2002.

[8]   Larsson, J.-O., "Higher Layer Key Exchange Techniques for Bluetooth Security," *Open Group Conf.*, Amsterdam, October 24, 2001.

[9]   van Oorschot, P. C., A. J. Menezes, and S. A. Vanstone, *Handbook of Applied Cryptography*, Boca Raton, FL: CRC Press, 1997.

[10] Jain, S. K., P. B. Bhattacharya, and S. R. Nagpaul, *Basic Abstract Algebra*, Cambridge: Cambridge University Press, 1986.

[11] NIST, *FIPS 180-1, Secure Hash Standard*, National Technical Information Service, Springfield, VA, April 1995.

[12] Simmons, G. J., "A Survey of Information Authentication," in G. J. Simmons, (ed.), *Contemporary Cryptology, The Science of Information Integrity*, New York: IEEE Press, 1992, pp. 379–420.

[13] Reed, I. S., and G. Solomon, "Polynomial Codes over Certain Finite Fields," *J. Society for Industrial and Applied Mathematics*, Vol. 8, 1960, pp. 300–304.

[14] Menezes, A. J., *Elliptic Curve Public Key Cryptosystems*, Dordrecht: Kluwer, 1993.

[15] Bluetooth Special Interest Group, *Specification of the Bluetooth System, Version 1.1, Profiles, Part K:10 Object Exchange Profile*, February 2001.

[16] Bluetooth Special Interest Group, *Specification of the Bluetooth System, Version 1.0, Personal Area Networking Profile,* February 2003.

[17] Bunk, L., and J. Vollbrecht, *PPP Extensible Authentication Protocol (EAP), RFC 2284,* March 1998.

[18] IEEE, *IEEE Std., 802.1x-2001, Version 2001, Port-Based Network Access Control,* June 2001.

[19] IEEE, *Standard Specifications for Public Key Cryptography, IEEE Std. 1353-2000,* 2000.

[20] ANSI, *Public Key Cryptography for the Financial Services Industry: Key Agreement and Key Transport Using Elliptic Curve Cryptography, ANSI X.9.63, 2001,* 2001.

[21] Blake-Wilson, S., "Higher Layer Key Exchange in Bluetooth," manuscript, private communication, 2001.

[22] Bluetooth Special Interest Group, *Specification of the Bluetooth System, Version 1.0, Bluetooth Network Encapsulation Protocol (BNEP) Specification,* February 2003.

[23] Kohl, J., and C. Neuman, *The Kerberos Network Authentication Service (V5), RFC 1510,* September 1993.

[24] Aboba, B., and D. Simon, *PPP EAP TLS Authentication Protocol, RFC 2716,* October 1999.

[25] Dierks, T., and C. Allen, *The TLS Protocol, Version 1.0, RFC 2246,* January 1999.

[26] Kent, S., and R. Atkinson, *IP Encapsulating Security Payload (ESP), RFC 1827,* November 1998.

[27] Kent, S., and R. Atkinson, *IP Authentication Header, RFC 2402,* November 1998.

[28] Gehrmann, C., and K. Nyberg, "Security in Personal Area Networks," in *Security for Mobility,* Herts: IEE, 2004.

[29] Mitchell, C., et al, "D13, Annex 3, wp3—Final Technical Report," Report IST-2000-25250, IST project SHAMAN, 2002.

[30] Mitchell, C., and R. Schaffelhofer, "The Personal PKI," in *Security for Mobility,* Herts: IEE, 2004.

[31] "Information Technology—Open System Interconnection—The Directory: Authentication Framework," *ISO/IEC 9594-8,* 1995.

[32] RSA Data Security Inc., Redwood City, CA, *PKCS #10: Certification Request Syntax Standard, v1.7,* 2000.

10

Security for Bluetooth Applications

So far we have described the basic Bluetooth security mechanisms and enhancements/extensions to these basic mechanisms. Exactly how one should use (or not use) Bluetooth security will depend on the application. Some applications are more security sensitive than others and might need special care in their security design. In this chapter we discuss how to use the different security mechanisms described for three different Bluetooth applications:

1. Headset;
2. Network access;
3. SIM access.

These applications do not at all cover all possible applications or profiles that are part of the Bluetooth specification. However, we think that the security problems one faces when implementing security for these applications are quite typical for most Bluetooth applications. When discussing how to provide security for the chosen set of applications, we show how one would benefit from using the enhancements described in Chapters 8 and 9, respectively. Hence, some of the implementation suggestions given in this chapter are not possible to realize using only the standard Bluetooth security mechanisms. The reason for including some enhancements in the description is to illustrate how one would benefit from the improvements.

The recommendations and analysis we provide for the headset and network access applications are partly covered in the Bluetooth security white paper [1] provided by the Bluetooth SIG. The network access security solution we show here is partly described in [2].

10.1 Headset

The Bluetooth specification contains a headset profile [3]. This profile is used for headset connections to, for example, mobile phones and laptops. Here we describe security solutions and usage for the Bluetooth headset profile. Bluetooth baseband security has been designed for personal devices, such as a headset, and the link level authentication and confidentiality protection is well suited for the protection of the headset application. The security association is used to authenticate and encrypt all communication between two Bluetooth wireless devices. In addition to this, a suitable implementation of Bluetooth Security and Bluetooth pass-key usage can prevent illegal use of a stolen headset. We will give a protocol implementation example with this property.

The standard Bluetooth pairing is rather weak, as we showed in Section 7.3. The improved pairing of Section 9.1 overcomes these weaknesses, and we have here chosen to base our description on availability of the improved pairing. However, the same security model and principles that we describe here can be used with the standard pairing mechanism (see Chapter 3). This will result in a less secure but otherwise similar implementation.

10.1.1 Headset security model

The dependencies between the different profiles are shown in Figure 1.7 in Chapter 1. As illustrated in the figure, the headset profile depends both on the serial profile and the GAP. The GAP defines the basic pairing and security behavior for most profiles, as well as for the headset profile. A typical headset configuration consists of two devices, a headset (HS) and an *audio gateway* (AG), as shown in Figure 10.1. The AG is typically a cellular phone, laptop, PC, or any type of audio-playing device, such as a radio and CD player. To protect the wireless channel from eavesdropping, it is recommended that communication between the HS and AG is protected by the Bluetooth authentication and encryption mechanisms. How and when to apply authentication and encryption is determined by policy rules that can be controlled and enforced by a security manager, as was discussed in Chapter 6.

In order to set up secure connections, the HS and AG need to store the necessary Bluetooth pass-keys and link keys. Since the HS usually does not have a user interface, it is appropriate to assume that an external device, such as the AG, may control some of the basic settings of the HS. This includes things like volume settings, handling the list of approved devices to be connected, and changing pass-key value. The HS security policy prescribes authentication and encryption settings, but also the access rules. It is the access policy that determines which audio connections are allowed and which devices are allowed to do remote control (including control of the security policies themselves).

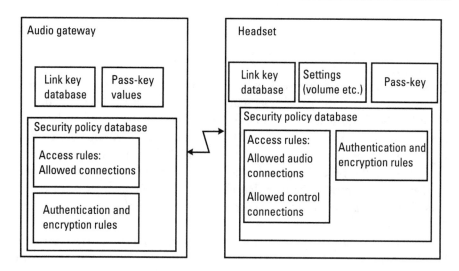

Figure 10.1 Headset security model.

The AG might be used for several other applications in addition to audio. Different security policies may apply for the different applications and connections. Hence, it is most likely that the AG operates in security mode 2, since this mode allows the most flexible security. Obviously, it is possible for both units to operate in security mode 1 as well. However, this would allow an eavesdropper to record the audio communication to the headset, which is not acceptable to most users.

Since the HS is a limited device, the security policy configuration should be kept as simple as possible. This means that security mode 3 is very suitable for the HS. In principle, security mode 2 can also be used, even if that implies a slightly higher implementation complexity. Authentication shall be required each time at connection setup. This implies that in order to get access, an AG device must have been previously paired with the HS, or a pairing must take place. The pairing will only succeed if the AG knows the correct pass-key value (we discuss pass-key handling for headsets in more detail later on). If the HS is stolen, the thief will probably not know the pass-key and will not succeed to connect to the HS with another AG. Consequently, some protection against illegal use of a stolen HS is provided.

10.1.2 Pass-key and key management

Normally, an HS does not contain an especially advanced user interface. Accordingly, it might be cumbersome, or even impossible, for the user to enter a new Bluetooth pass-key value into the HS for each pairing. Hence, a fixed Bluetooth pass-key in the HS is reasonable. A fixed pass-key has security drawbacks, since the probability that someone will find out the secret value is higher for a pass-key that is never changed than for a frequently updated pass-key. Consequently, higher security is obtained if the fixed pass-key is also changed regularly. There is no simple answer to what "regularly" means, as it depends on such things as how often the pass-key is actually used and if it has been disclosed to someone else. In principle, the more frequent changes, the better. It should be possible to control the settings of the HS from the AG. An external device like a PDA, a laptop, or some other controlling unit might have a better user interface, thus allowing the Bluetooth pass-key to be changed swiftly. Naturally, the HS implementation must make sure that changing the Bluetooth pass-key is only possible over an authenticated and encrypted Bluetooth link, or by using a wired connection.

In Chapter 9 we described improved pairing using relatively short pass-keys and MACs. In the improved pairing scheme, the probability of a successful attack depends solely on the length of the pass-key value and the risk for off-line attacks is eliminated. Furthermore, no additional information on the pass-key value is disclosed, even if the same pass-key value is used for several pairings. Hence, the solution gives good security also when fixed pass-keys are used. Consequently, the improved pairing is suitable for the HS application case. This means that the involved AG and HS both must support *DH key agreement computations* as well as *MAC-based pairing*. However, in order to use the improved pairing, either the HS and AG must support the improved pairing on the baseband level or none of the devices can operate in security mode 3. This is because a device in security mode 3 demands authentication during connection setup, and thus it will not be possible to do the pairing on a higher layer. Hence, for interoperability reasons, as long as the improved pairing is not a standard Bluetooth feature, it cannot be directly used.

Using the improved pairing approach provides better security than the conventional Bluetooth pairing. In the improved pairing case, a new pass-key can be generated by letting a controlling AG or HS randomly select a new MAC key and compute the new corresponding MAC value. If the standard Bluetooth pairing mechanism is used, randomly generated initial Bluetooth pass-keys that are unique for each HS should be used. If the Bluetooth pass-key for a headset can be changed, it might be necessary to allow someone with physical access to the HS to reset the HS to its original (factory preset) pass-key. This makes it possible for someone to continue to use a headset even if the user loses or forgets the current Bluetooth passkey, but has kept a copy of the (factory preset) pass-key. Note that a resettable pass-key will still give protection against theft, provided that HSs are not shipped with the same original (factory preset) pass-key.

Even better security is achieved if pairing of an AG with an HS only is allowed when the user has explicitly set the HS into pairable mode. Pairing in a public place, such as a point of sale, is discouraged when using the ordinary pairing procedure, as there is much greater risk that a subversive unit may intercept the key exchange. The improved pairing procedure does not have this weakness.

The HS should use combination keys for its connections. The HS should store the combination keys in nonvolatile memory. Higher security is provided if this memory is also tamper resistant. Clearly, the same is also true for the AG.

10.1.3 Example

Finally, we give a pairing and connection example for the headset application. There are several ways of implementing HS security and control. Here, we assume that we use the baseband security functions in combination with the improved pairing procedure that we described in Chapter 9. The improved pairing is currently not part of the Bluetooth standard. However, since better security is provided with the improved pairing, we have nonetheless chosen in this example to assume that this enhancement is available. We illustrate how to secure a headset through a user scenario:

> Assume a new HS is delivered to a customer. The customer would like to use the HS together with a mobile phone acting as the AG. The HS is delivered with a preset pass-key known to the customer. This pass-key is a combination of a MAC key and a MAC as described in Section 9.1. We assume that HS security is implemented using security mode 2 with authentication and encryption required for all connections.

In this scenario, the following steps describe user interactions, mobile phone to HS interactions, and security calculations needed before the customer is able to use the HS together with the mobile phone:

1. The customer sets the HS into discoverable and pairable mode by pressing a button on the HS.

2. The HS indicates to the user that it is ready for pairing.

3. The customer prepares the mobile phone for discovery of a new Bluetooth HS device.

4. The phone performs a Bluetooth inquiry and gets a response from the HS and a Bluetooth connection is established.

5. The HS demands authentication of the AG (phone).

6. Both the HS and the AG detect that they do not have any link key that can be used for the connection and the improved pairing procedure is started.

7. The HS has a stored DH public key value, g^a, that it sends to the AG.

8. The AG ask the user to enter the secret pass-key for the HS. It consists of the MAC key, l, and the corresponding MAC value, t.

9. The AG checks that the received DH public value $g^{a'}$ matches t (the MAC) for the given key l that the user entered.

10. The AG generates a second DH key b and the corresponding DH public key g^b and calculates the DH shared secret, $K = (g^{a'})b$.

11. The AG uses the key K to encrypt the string l using an agreed-on secure encryption function b' (which could be a simple one-time pad) and sends g^b and $E_K(l)$ to the HS.

12. Device HS receives the $g^{b'}$ and $E_K(l)'$ strings. The HS derives the DH key $K' = (g^{b'})^a$ and decrypts the l' using the key K'. If l' matches the stored string, l, then K' is accepted as a combination key between the HS and the AG.

13. The new link key between the HS and the telephone is stored in non-volatile memory in both the AG and the HS unit.

14. The HS and AG perform mutual baseband authentication based on K as the link key and switch to an encrypted connection.

15. The customer switches the HS out of the discoverable and pairable mode so it will no longer accept any new inquiries or pairing requests.

At this point, the HS will only accept connections from a phone with which it has been paired. From all other devices, it will request a pairing. The HS will require authentication and encryption before any LMP channel setup can be completed. If the HS is stolen, the illegitimate user can try to set up a connection with it. This is prevented by mandating authentication. If the HS owner wants to transfer the HS to another user to be used in connection with a different phone, for example, if the owner is selling the HS, then the new user should change the pass-key of the HS and not disclose the new key to the old owner. There is no security risk for the HS by keeping the old DH public and private key values for new key exchanges, since the public DH key gives no information on the private key. Next, a pass-key update sample procedure is described:

1. The user opens a special external device control menu on a mobile phone (AG) and asks it to connect to the HS.

2. Using a dedicated control protocol, the AG contacts the HS and establishes a control connection. Authentication is performed and encryption is switched on before the connection is established.

3. Using a dedicated menu on the AG, the user opts to change the fixed pass-key of the HS. The phone asks the user to enter the old pass-key.

4. The AG sends a request to the HS for changing the pass-key. Together with the request, the AG also sends the old pass-key. A dedicated protocol between the AG and HS is used for this purpose.

5. The HS checks the received pass-key and compared it with the existing pass-key. If they match, the HS generates a new MAC key, l. The key and the DH public value of the HS is used to calculate the new corresponding MAC, t. The string (l, t) will be the new pass-key of the HS. The old pass-key is deleted.

6. The HS sends the new pass-key value to the AG.

7. The AG either just displays the new pass-key to the user or it securely stores it in protected memory in the AG.

8. The AG might now request the HS to delete all old link keys.

From now on, when the user sets the HS into pairing mode, it will only accept a pairing with the new pass-key. It is advisable to store the pass-key for the exceptional case that a new pairing with the HS is required, for example, if the link key gets destroyed due to a malfunction of the system. The user must keep the new pass-key in a secure place.

10.2 Network access

Next we describe a security solution for network access. Network access to an IP network in Bluetooth is provided through the PAN profile [4]. The PAN isbuilt upon the BNEP [5] specification, which defines the encapsulation of Ethernet packets allowing direct LAN access through a *network access point* (NAcP).

Here we discuss how to secure access based on the PAN profile for a scenario where a user subscribes to and pays for network access services through a network access service provider. Once the user has subscribed to the service, it will be possible to connect a device to a LAN run by the service provider through Bluetooth access points that have been set up by the access service provider. We describe a solution partly based on the improved pairing we introduced in Chapter 9. This means that the involved terminals and access points support DH key agreement computations as well as the MAC-based pairing. The solution also utilizes the alias authentication mechanism that was described in Chapter 8. Alias authentication and the DH-based pairing are particularly suitable for the network access scenario, and its use here illustrates some of the advantages with the enhancements we have introduced. It is hard to build a good network access security solution using only the standard Bluetooth security mechanisms, and some additional features are needed. An alternative to the solution we describe here is to use an IEEE 802.1X–based approach [6] (see Section 9.2).

We are considering a situation where a Bluetooth *data terminal* (DT) can move around and access several different NAcPs belonging to the same access service provider. In order to be user friendly, manual configuration at each new connection setup should be avoided. One possible security principle for the architecture would be to use totally open (from a security point of view) access points that can be accessed by anybody. But, more likely, the service provider would like to restrict the access. Furthermore, Bluetooth users would like to be sure that they connect to the correct access point and that the traffic sent over the Bluetooth radio interface is not eavesdropped on.

10.2.1 Common access keys

We suggest using a security architecture built around a *common access key* (CAK) concept that is new within Bluetooth but is used in other technologies. A CAK is a link key that is not limited to one particular link, but rather is used for all links that are established toward a particular network. Thus, a user will have one CAK for all access points belonging to that particular network. Moreover, different users will have different CAKs to the same network and a user will need different CAKs for different networks.

By using CAKs we can, with only minor changes, use the baseband security mechanism also for the access point roaming scenario. If the network uses alias authentication (see Section 8.5), it will be possible for the DT to find the right CAK to use for the connection directly on the baseband level (note that alias authentication can be used independently of the rest of the anonymity mode features). In this case, all NAcPs will use the same alias address. This allows fast connections without user interaction, as described in Section 10.2.5. We assume that before a unit subscribes to a new service, a CAK for that particular service is generated. It is possible for the user to force a unit to only use ordinary combination keys for some connections, while it still might allow CAKs for other type of connections. For example, the key database in the DT can look like Table 10.1.

This is similar to the database structure discussed in Section 3.7.

In the table, records for combination keys have the device address filled with the corresponding Bluetooth unit address. The CAKs have the address field filled with alias address of the network. In the example, the two first keys are CAKs while the second two are ordinary combination keys.

If the device is accessing the network in anonymity mode, an additional address field with its own alias address shall be added to the key database. (This is not shown in Table 10.1.)

Table 10.1

Link Key Data Base Example with CAKs

Service	Alias or Device Address	Usage	Key	Key Type
Service provider A	A32FF81ACC10	PAN	1B4D5698AE374FDE B8390912463DFE3A	CAK
Service provider B	478AEB2B895C	PAN	FE729425BC9A95D3 9132BDE275917823	CAK
Any	A5EE29667190	Always	091827AD41D4E48D 29CBE82615D18490	C*
⋮	⋮	⋮	⋮	⋮
Any	068935F6B3E2	Always	126304467592CD71 FF19B4428133AD8E	C*

*Indicates a combination key.

10.2.2 Security architecture

We suggest an architecture where the baseband authentication and encryption are used to protect the access link. The architecture can be implemented using the improved pairing with DH key exchange for the initial access, and this description will be based on the improved pairing. The Bluetooth baseband authentication is used to make sure that only legitimate users are able to connect to the LAN. We distinguish between three different situations (from the DT point of view):

1. *Network service subscription:* The user needs to do some action in order to subscribe to the network service and possibly also make an initial payment.

2. *Initial network connection:* Initially, a DT tries to connect to a network to which it has not been connected previously. Hence, a link key must be exchanged.

3. *Subsequent access to NAcPs:* Here we utilize the CAK concept to allow convenient access to different NAcPs. This means that subsequent connections are handled automatically without any interaction with higher layer security mechanisms.

10.2.3 Network service subscription

Next we describe how to create the necessary initial trust relation. Assume a user would like to register a DT for getting LAN access through NAcPs installed by a certain LAN access service provider or organization. This can be done, for example, using one of the following two options:

1. The user registers the DT at the LAN access provider through some regular (non-Bluetooth) procedure (e.g., phone, office, Web).

2. The user is getting LAN through the user's own organization and the DT needs some preconfiguration in order to be allowed to access the network through NAcPs.

We assume that when a DT user subscribes to a LAN access service, that user gets a unique ID that identifies the service provider. Along with the ID, the user receives a secret pass-key. The pass-key is built of a combined secret key and the corresponding MAC according to the improved pairing principles described in Chapter 9. The secret key part of the pass-key needs to be generated independently for each DT subscriber in the LAN by the LAN access service provider using a secure random generator. However, we assume that the network uses the same DH keys for all different DT subscribers. In order to not compromise security, the service provider must store private DH keys in a central database. For convenience, the public DH key can also be stored in the same repository.

The DT user (or someone acting on behalf of the DT user) needs to enter the pass-key manually into the device, in its protected (through encryption or tamper-resistant storage) DT service database. The DT network subscription database entry consists of two values:

1. LAN access service ID;

2. Pass-key for the particular LAN access service.

At registration, the user also receives a unique DT ID from the LAN access provider. This ID has nothing to do with the *BD_ADDR* of either the DT or the access points. As part of the subscription, the LAN access provider needs to store the pass-key and corresponding DT ID in a central secure database. Preferably, this can be the same server that also stores the DH secret key for the network. To summarize, the following parameters must be kept in a central secure server by the service provider:

- Network DH secret and public keys;

- DT ID;

- The pass-keys corresponding to the different DT IDs.

All NAcPs in the access network need to have secure access and connection to this database, as illustrated in Figure 10.2. The access and connection to the database can be secured by any standard method, like TLS [7] or IPsec [8].

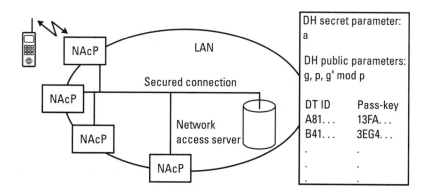

Figure 10.2 LAN with access points and central secure access server.

10.2.4 Initial connection

Once the DT has got the service ID and pass-key configuration, it will be able to connect to the network. This can be done in several different ways. We will give a sample procedure. It is a rough description of the protocol and interactions with the network, and the details are left out. Figure 10.3 illustrates the different actions.

Below, the different steps are outlined:

1. The DT connects to the NAcP using the Bluetooth inquiry/paging procedure.

2. The DT acts as a service discovery protocol (SDP) client and searches for the LAN access service record on the NAcP. The DT receives the service ID of the LAN service provider. The NAcP may perform a similar service discovery sequence on the DT to obtain the DT ID.

3. The DT checks that it knows the service ID received over the SDP protocol. Otherwise, the DT interrupts the connection procedure.

4. The DT asks the internal service database for the pass-key corresponding to the service ID.

5. The corresponding pass-key in the internal database is returned to the DT.

6. The NAcP uses a dedicated protocol to send the public key of the network together with the alias address of the network to the DT. The alias address is needed by the DT in order to look up the correct link key for authentication of the access points at the Bluetooth link level.

7. The DT validates the DH value that it receives using the pass-key it found in step 5 (see Section 8.5 for the details).

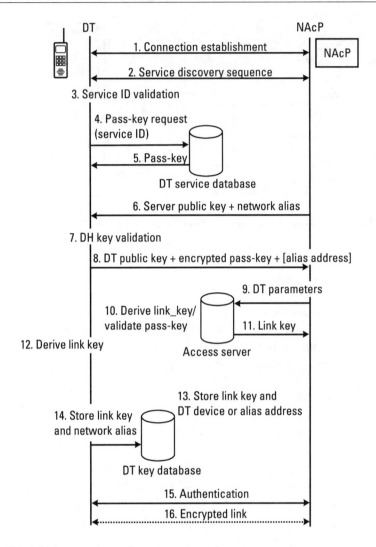

Figure 10.3 Initial connection to the access network.

8. The DT sends its own public DH key together with an encrypted pass-key and optionally an alias address (if the DT wants to be anonymous) to the NAcP.

9. The NAcP connects to the access server through a secure connection and sends the parameters it received in step 8 together with the DT ID to the access server.

10. The access server derives the DH shared secret, decrypts the pass-key, and verifies it against the pass-key value corresponding to the received

DT ID, which is stored in its database. The access server derives a Bluetooth link key from the DH shared secret.

11. The access server returns the link key derived in step 10 to the NAcP.

12. The DT also calculates the DH shared secret and derives a link key from it.

13. The access server stores the new link key together with the DT Bluetooth address (fixed or alias) in its database.

14. The DT stores the new link key as a CAK together with the network alias address in the DT key database.

15. The DT and NAcP perform a mutual baseband authentication using the newly derived link key.

16. Optionally the Bluetooth link is encrypted.

Through the procedure described above, both the network and the DT are equipped with the necessary security parameters for making subsequent access to the network quick and convenient.

10.2.5 Subsequent access to NAcPs

Finally, we describe how subsequent access can be made securely and efficiently using the CAK and alias authentication. The procedure works fine for the DT with both security mode 2 and security mode 3. For subsequent access, the NAcPs could also use security mode 3. However, security mode 3 does not work well with the initial access procedure, and security mode 2 is the preferred mode of operation for the NAcPs. If the DT connects to the LAN for the fist time, authentication and encryption are performed according to the description in Section 10.2.4. For all other cases, the procedure is as described in Figure 10.4.

Below, the different steps of the secure connection establishment are outlined:

1. The DT connects to the NAcP using the Bluetooth inquiry/paging procedure.

2. The NAcP sends its alias address to the DT through a dedicated LM command (see Section 8.5 in Chapter 8 for the details).

3. The DT optionally (if it is anonymous) also sends its alias address to the NAcP.

4. The DT uses the alias address to find the right CAK in its key database.

5. The DT finds the link key (CAK) to use for the connection.

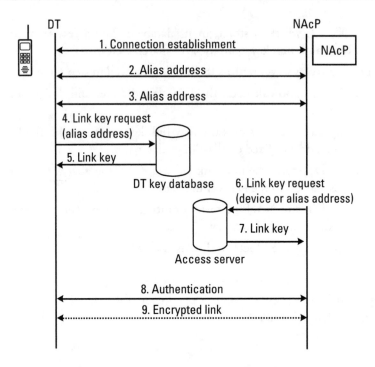

Figure 10.4 Subsequent access to the network.

6. The NAcP connects to the access server through a secure connection and requests the link key for the received device or alias address.

7. The access server finds the requested link key and returns the link to the NAcP.

8. The DT and NAcP perform a mutual baseband authentication using the found link key.

9. Optionally, the Bluetooth link is encrypted.

The procedure described above completes the secure connection establishment between the DT and the NAcP. If the DT runs in anonymous mode, it may also choose to update its alias address after authentication and encryption are enabled. Then the NAcP must send the updated alias address to the access server. The NAcP, on the other hand, does not have any anonymity requirement and can always keep the same alias.

The procedure in Figure 10.4 can be repeated whenever the DT moves and would like to connect to a new NAcP. In this way, secure roaming between access points is achieved.

10.3 SIM access

In this section we will discuss security issues and solutions for remote access to a *subscription identity module* (SIM) [9] over a Bluetooth connection. The SIM access application is provided by a Bluetooth profile. A SIM card is an integrated circuit card used in the GSM mobile telephony system. It is used to hold subscriber information. This information in turn is used to securely connect a mobile phone to a cellular GSM network and it makes it possible for the mobile network operator to securely identify subscribers attaching to the network. Consequently, it also allows the operator to bill the use of mobile network services. The SIM interface is specified in [9] and the card interface follows the ISO/IEC 7816-3 standard [10]. A SIM can be used for a large variety of services offered by GSM service providers.

We start this section by giving a short overview of the SIM access profile. Next, security-related problems and solutions for SIM access are discussed.

10.3.1 The SIM access profile

The Bluetooth SIM access profile defines procedures and protocols for access to a remote SIM over a Bluetooth serial port (RFCOMM) connection. The protocol stack is illustrated in Figure 10.5.

The SIM access messages consists of a header and a payload. The header describes the type and the number of parameters transferred in the message. Messages have been defined for control of the SIM card remotely and to transfer SIM card messages. Two different roles are defined in the profile:

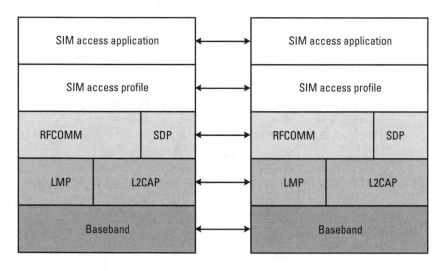

Figure 10.5 The SIM access profile communication stack.

1. SIM access client;
2. SIM access server.

The SIM access client uses the SIM access profile to connect to another device, the SIM access server, over Bluetooth. The server is the device with the SIM card reader and SIM card attached. A typical usage scenario is illustrated in Figure 10.6. In this scenario, a laptop is connected to a wireless network (WLAN or cellular network). A SIM is needed for subscriber authentication in the wireless network. The laptop does not have a smart card reader and will need to use the phone with a SIM for network access. The SIM card that is needed for the access resides in the phone, and the laptop uses the SIM access profile to access it.

10.3.2 Securing SIM access

The SIM is used for security critical services. The card holds secret keys and subscriber information that must be well protected. The smart card technology provides tamper resistance protection. However, the interface to the card is not protected in any other way than that the card is "opened" with a secret PIN. Once the card is opened, it will perform most tasks that are requested (some tasks may require a second PIN to be entered). The SIM access profile allows the card "interface" to be extended over the Bluetooth link. Consequently, it is very important that the wireless link is well protected. We will describe the security mechanism mandated by the profile [11] and also discuss additional security measures that SIM access profile implementers should take.

SIM access mandates the following:

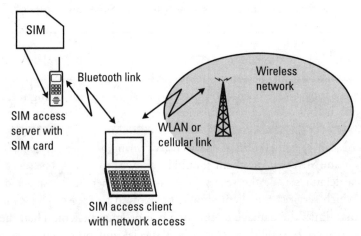

Figure 10.6 SIM access profile usage scenario.

- Security mode 2 or 3 shall be used.

- The client and server must be paired before they set up a SIM access connection.

- A pass-key with length of at least 16 decimal digits shall be used at the pairing. Furthermore, fixed pass-keys are not allowed.

- The server shall always authenticate the client.

- The Bluetooth link between the client and server shall always be encrypted and the key length shall be at least 64 bits.

These requirements ensure a good basic security level for the SIM access connection, since it is not so easy to do a brute force attack on a 16-digit pass-key. Furthermore, the Bluetooth authentication and encryption algorithms are sufficiently strong (see Chapter 7). However, a 64-bit encryption key is a little bit too short, and whenever possible a 128-bit key is recommended instead. Entering a 16-digit pass-key can be cumbersome for the user. Actually, users tend to choose low entropy pass-key values when such a long string as 16 digits is required. A better approach than having the user choose the pass-key is to let the server generate the pass-key value and display it to the user. The user then enters the same value into the client device. The pass-key needs to be generated by choosing the pass-key bits uniformly and at random. The improved pairing that we described in Chapter 9 does not have the problem with entering a long pass-key and suits well also for the SIM access profile.

The security required by the SIM access profile gives the necessary basic protection for the message exchange between the client and server. However, there are additional security measures that need to be taken in order to avoid introducing security holes in the SIM access implementation. One of the problems is that in an implementation that just follows the specification, all messages from the client to the server will be accepted and forwarded to the SIM. This is a potential security risk for the sensitive functions in the subscription module. All functions will be available for the remote device, that is, the SIM access client. This device might have been compromised in some way or it might have been infected by a virus or other harmful software. Hence, there must be a way for the server to restrict the access to the subscription module.

This can be achieved if, at the security pairing, the server selects the set of services in the SIM that the client should be allowed to access. The set of services can be a default set, or the server may ask the owner of the server device to decide which services the client should be allowed to access. This should be a subset that limits the damage in case of a compromised client. Then the record of allowed services should be stored in a special and protected access control database. When the client has been authenticated against the server, a filtering

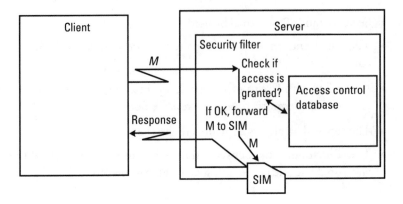

Figure 10.7 Access control to a SIM.

process or a security filter will check all messages from the client to the subscription module, as is illustrated in Figure 10.7. The filter makes sure that only messages allowed according to the access database are forwarded to the subscription module.

Another security problem with the SIM access profile is that the PIN needed to open the SIM is sent from the client to the server. This means that if the client device is untrusted or infected by malicious software, the PIN for the card can be intercepted by a third party. To avoid this, the access filter in Figure 10.7 shall not accept PIN commands from the client, but demand the SIM to be opened from the server device. Then the user must enter the SIM PIN into the trusted server device before the SIM access profile connection is set up. Clearly, this implies that a proper input interface must be present at the SIM access server.

References

[1]   Bluetooth Special Interest Group, *Bluetooth Security White Paper*, Version 1.0, 19 April 2002.

[2]   Gehrmann, C., and K. Nyberg, "Enhancements to Bluetooth Baseband Security," *Proc. Nordsec 2001*, Copenhagen, November 2001, pp. 39–53.

[3]   Bluetooth Special Interest Group, *Specification of the Bluetooth System, Version 1.1, Profiles, Part K:6 Headset Profile*, February 2001.

[4]   Bluetooth Special Interest Group, *Specification of the Bluetooth System, Version 1.0, Personal Area Networking Profile*, February 2003.

[5]   Bluetooth Special Interest Group, *Specification of the Bluetooth System, Version 1.0, Bluetooth Network Encapsulation Protocol (BNEP) Specification*, February 2003.

[6] IEEE, *IEEE Std., 802.1x-2001, Version 2001, Port-Based Network Access Control,* June 2001.

[7] Dierks, T., and C. Allen, *The TLS Protocol, Version 1.0, RFC 2246,* January 1999.

[8] Kent, S., and R. Atkinson, *IP Encapsulating Security Payload (ESP), RFC 1827,* November 1998.

[9] 3rd Generation Partnership Programme, *3GPP TS 11.11, Specification of the Subscriber Identity Module Mobile Equipment (SIM-ME) Interface, Version 8.10.0,* September 2003.

[10] International Organization for Standardization, *ISO/IEC 7816-3 Information Technology—Identification Cards Integrated Circuit(s) Cards with Contacts—Part 3: Electronic Signals and Transmission Protocols,* 2nd ed., 1997.

[11] Bluetooth Special Interest Group, *Specification of the Bluetooth System, Version 0.95, SIM Access Profile Specification,* June 2002.

Glossary

Throughout the book, several terms have been used. Some are commonly used within the field of security research, while other terms are specifically related to Bluetooth. Below we give short definitions for all of these.

Active wiretapper   A wiretapper that is capable of injecting and modifying messages at will.

Ciphertext   Data protected through the use of encipherment. The semantic context of the resulting data is not available.

Claimant   The entity that claims to be a specific peer entity, that is, claiming a specific identity.

Connectable   A Bluetooth device that regularly performs a page scan, and therefore can be reached by other devices knowing its device address.

Denial-of-service (DoS) attack   The prevention of authorized access to resources or the delaying of time-critical operations. The resulting system degradation can, for example, be the result of the system being fully occupied by handling bogus connection requests.

Discoverable   A Bluetooth device that regularly performs inquiry scanning and therefore can be detected by other devices.

Eavesdropper   See *passive wiretapper.*

Fixed pass-key   A pass-key that cannot be arbitrarily chosen at the pairing instance.

Impersonation attack   An attack whereby the attacker sends data and claims that the data originates from another entity.

Key management   The generation, storage, distribution, deletion, archiving, and application of keys in accordance with a security policy.

Known plaintext attack   Attack on a ciphering system using knowledge of ciphertext data and the matching cleartext.

Pairable   A Bluetooth device for which the security policy is to accept pairing attempts.

Passive wiretapper   A person that wiretaps a link by making a copy of the data that is sent via the link. The state of the system is not changed.

Peer-entity authentication   The corroboration that a peer entity in an association is the one claimed.

Plaintext   Intelligible data for which the semantic context of the resulting data is available.

Security policy   The set of criteria for the provision of security services.

Trusted device   A remote device with which a long-lasting security relation has been established. A trusted device is given unconditional access to all services running on the local device after it has been successfully authenticated.

Untrusted device   A remote device with which a temporary or a long-lasting security relation has been established. An untrusted device does not get unconditional access to services running on the local device; authentication as well as authorization is required.

Variable pass-key   A pass-key that can be arbitrarily chosen at the pairing instance.

Verifier   The entity that challenges another entity for its claimed identity.

List of Acronyms and Abbreviations

Here we list the acronyms and abbreviations used in the book. In cases for which it is not obvious what the meaning of the listed item is, a short explanation has also been provided.

ACL Asynchronous connection-oriented (logical transport).

ACO Authenticated ciphering offset. A parameter binding devices to a particular authentication event.

AES Advanced Encryption Standard

AG Audio gateway. A mobile phone or other outloud-playing device (connected to a headset).

BB Baseband. This is the lowest layer of the Bluetooth specification.

BD_ADDR Bluetooth device address

BER Bit error rate. Average probability that a received bit is erroneous.

BNEP Bluetooth network encapsulation protocol. Emulation of Ethernet over Bluetooth links.

CA Certificate authority. Trusted issuer of certificates.

CAC Channel access code. A code derived from the master device address in a Bluetooth connection

CAK Common access key. A common key that can be used when connecting to different access points belonging to a particular network provider.

CID Channel identifier. End points at an L2CAP channel.

COF Ciphering offset. Additional secret input to ciphering key generation procedure.

CPU Central processing unit

CRC Cyclic redundancy check. A checksum added to the payload by the sender that the receiver can use to detect transmission errors.

DAC Device access code

DH Diffie-Hellman. The name of the first public key exchange scheme.

DoS Denial of service

DSP Digital signal processor

DT Data terminal

EAP Extensible authentication protocol. An authentication protocol standardized by the IETF organization.

EAPOL EAP encapsulation over LANs

ECDH Elliptic-curve Diffie-Hellman

eSCO Enhanced synchronous connection-oriented. A logical channel for transport of prioritized synchronous user data.

FEC Forward error correction. Another notion for an error correcting code.

FH Frequency hopping

FHS Frequency hop synchronization

GAP   Generic access profile. A Bluetooth profile that determines common connection handling functions for all other Bluetooth profiles.

GSM   Global Mobile System

HC   Host controller

HCI   Host controller interface

HS   Headset

IAC   Inquiry access code

ICC   Integrated circuit card

ID   Identifier

IEEE   Institute of Electrical and Electronics Engineers. A nonprofit technical professional association for engineers in this area.

IETF   Internet Engineering Task Force

IIR   Infinite impulse response

IKE   Internet key exchange. An IETF protocol used to authenticate IP connections and to exchange IPSEC keys.

IP   Internet protocol.

IPSEC   IP security protocol. An IETF security protocol used to protect IP packets.

ISM   Industrial, scientific, and medical. A part of the radio spectrum reserved for these kinds of applications.

L2CAP   Logical link communication and adaptation protocol.

LAN   Local area network

LAP   Lower address part. Bits 0 to 23 of the unique 48-bit IEEE device address.

LC Link controller. Entity that implements the baseband protocol and procedures.

LFSR Linear feedback shift register

LM Link manager. Entity that sets up and maintains the Bluetooth link.

LMP Link manager protocol

LSB Least significant bit

LT_ADDR Logical transport address. A logical 3-bit address assigned to each slave in a piconet.

MAC Message authentication code

MANA Manual authentication

MSB Most significant bit

NAcP Network access point

NAP Nonsignificant address part. Bits 32 to 47 of the unique 48-bit IEEE device address.

OBEX Object exchange

OpCode Operation code_A code used to identify different types of PDUs.

PAN Personal area network

PCD Personal certification device

PDA Personal digital assistant

PDU Protocol data unit

PIN Personal identification number

PKI Public key infrastructure

PSM Protocol/service multiplexor. An identifier used by L2CAP during channel establishment to route the connection request to the right upper layer protocol. Several protocols can be multiplexed over L2CAP.

QoS Quality of service. Defines the specific requirements on the link (e.g., with respect to bit rate, delay, latency) needed by certain applications.

RFCOMM A serial cable emulation protocol based on ETSI TS 07.10

RS-code Reed-Solomon code.

RSA Rivest, Shamir, and Adleman. The name of a public-key cryptosystem for both encryption and authentication.

SCO Synchronous connection-oriented. A logical channel for transport of synchronous user data.

SDP Service discovery protocol. A protocol for locating services provided by or available through a Bluetooth device.

SIG Special Interest Group. The organization owning the Bluetooth trademark, also responsible for the evolution of Bluetooth wireless technology.

SIM Subscription identity module. An ICC used in the GSM mobile telephony system. The module stores subscription and user data.

TCP Transmission control protocol. An IETF protocol for reliable IP communication.

TLS Transport layer security. An IETF security protocol used to authenticate peers, exchange keys, and protect TCP traffic.

UAP Upper address part. Bits 24 to 31 of the unique 48-bit IEEE device address.

UART Universal asynchronous receiver/transmitter. An integrated circuit used for serial communication with the transmitter and receiver clocked separately.

USB Universal serial bus

WLAN Wireless local area network

About the Authors

Christian Gehrmann received his M.Sc. in electrical engineering and his Ph.D. in information theory from Lund University, Sweden, in 1991 and 1997, respectively. He joined Ericsson in Stockholm in 1997. At Ericsson he has primarily been working with wireless network and terminal security research and standardization. Since 2002, he has held a senior specialist position in security architectures and protocols at Ericsson Mobile Platforms AB in Lund. He has published several research papers in the wireless personal area network security area and is a key contributor to the Bluetooth security improvements work. He was the chairman of the Bluetooth SIG Security Expert Group in 2001 and 2002.

Joakim Persson received his M.Sc. in computer engineering and his Ph.D. in information theory from Lund University, Sweden, in 1990 and 1996, respectively. He joined the research department at Ericsson Mobile Platforms AB in 1996, and since 1999 he has been a technical manager for the new technology section within this department. He has been working with Bluetooth since 1997 and is one of the key contributors to the baseband specification. As a member of the Radio Working Group of Bluetooth SIG, he has also been working with the evolution of the technology.

Ben Smeets is an Ericsson expert in security systems and data compression at Ericsson Mobile Platforms AB. He is a full professor of digital switching theory at Lund University and holds a Ph.D. and Docent degree, in digital techniques from Lund University and an M.Sc. in electrical engineering from Eindhoven University of Technology. At Ericsson Mobile Platforms he is guiding studies and implementation of security applications and basic security features in mobile devices. He also functions as an internal consultant on security aspects in digital systems design. In the academic sphere he is pursuing research in cryptology, particularly stream cipher analysis, and in information theory.

Index

Access control
  IEEE 802.1x port-based, 150–52
  L2CAP, 93
  SIM, 184
Active address, 123, 125–27
  defined, 125
  use of, 125
  See also Addresses
Addresses
  active, 123, 125–27
  alias, 123, 128
  fixed, 123, 124
  update, 134
  usage, 124–28
Ad hoc connectivity, 4, 20–22
  defined, 20
  scenario, 21
Advanced Encryption Standard (AES), 63
Algorithms, 65–80
  E_0, 74–79
  E_1, 70–71
  E_3, 73
  E_{21}, 71–72
  E_{22}, 72–73
  encryption, 32–34
  f8, 66
  selection, 65
Alias address, 123
  authentication, 128

  defined, 128
  exchange, 134–35
  format, 132
  use of, 131
  See also Addresses
Alias authentication, 131–32
  in asymmetric fashion, 132
  defined, 124, 131
  using, 131–32
Anonymity
  address changes for, 123
  inquiry and, 129
  providing, 123–38
Anonymity mode
  address update command, 134
  alias address exchange command, 134–35
  defined, 123
  fixed address exchange command, 135–36
  identification, 128
  LMP commands, 133–36
  overview, 123–24
Application security, 167–84
  headset, 168–73
  network access, 173–80
  SIM access, 181–84
Asymmetric mechanisms, 23
Asynchronous connection-oriented (ACL)
  links, 10
  packets, 12

Techniques and Applications of Digital Watermarking and Content Protection, Michael Arnold, Martin Schmucker, and Stephen D. Wolthusen

For further information on these and other Artech House titles, including previously considered out-of-print books now available through our In-Print-Forever® (IPF®) program, contact:

Artech House
685 Canton Street
Norwood, MA 02062
Phone: 781-769-9750
Fax: 781-769-6334
e-mail: artech@artechhouse.com

Artech House
46 Gillingham Street
London SW1V 1AH UK
Phone: +44 (0)20 7596-8750
Fax: +44 (0)20 7630-0166
e-mail: artech-uk@artechhouse.com

Find us on the World Wide Web at:
www.artechhouse.com

Recent Titles in the Artech House Computing Library

For further information on these and other Artech House titles, including previously considered out-of-print books now available through our In-Print-Forever® (IPF®) program, contact:

Artech House
685 Canton Street
Norwood, MA 02062
Phone: 781-769-9750
Fax: 781-769-6334
e-mail: artech@artechhouse.com

Artech House
46 Gillingham Street
London SW1V 1AH UK
Phone: +44 (0)20 7596-8750
Fax: +44 (0)20 7630-0166
e-mail: artech-uk@artechhouse.com

Find us on the World Wide Web at:
www.artechhouse.com

the master can decide which is the greatest common key length supported and request this to be used.

The *encryption mode* parameter of the LMP encryption mode req PDU determines whether to use encryption or not. If this mode is set to 0x1 or 0x2, encryption applies to individually addressed messages (point-to-point traffic). Additionally, if a temporary link key is used, broadcast messages are also encrypted; if a semipermanent link key is used, broadcast messages are not encrypted. Note that setting the encryption mode to 0x2 is not recommended from version 1.2. The mode is still part of the specification only to allow for backward compatibility with 1.1-compliant devices.

Consequently, the encryption mode parameter written by the HCI Write Encryption Mode command can only take the values 0x0 and 0x1.

Figure 5.1 depicts a message sequence chart describing different steps in setting up broadcast encryption as well as returning from broadcast to individual link encryption. For enabling of the master link key, the HCI Master Link Key command with Key_Flag set to 0x01 is issued by the master host.

The same random number must be used in all the LMP start encryption req commands; otherwise, different ciphering initialization values will cause problems once encryption is switched on. It is up to the host to decide whether to attempt broadcasting encrypted data when not all slaves are set to receive encrypted broadcast data, but the recommendation is not to do so.

If, for some rare necessary reason, the mutual authentication following the LMP temp rand and LMP temp key fails, the LM of the verifier should issue the detach procedure for that link. This will allow the procedure to succeed even though one of the devices may be erroneous.

[1]   Bluetooth Special Interest Group, *The Bluetooth Wireless Specification, Version 1.1*, February 2001.

[2]   Bluetooth Special Interest Group, *Specification of the Bluetooth System, Version 1.2, Core System Package*, November 2003.

Recent Titles in the Artech House Computer Security Series

Rolf Oppliger, Series Editor